Sons, Lovers, and Fathers:

Understanding Male Sexuality

Sons, Lovers, and Fathers:
Understanding Male Sexuality

Didier Dumas

Translated and adapted by:
Anne Trager
Christopher Fleischner

Jason Aronson Inc.
Northvale, New Jersey
London

Director of Editorial Production: Robert D. Hack

This book was set in 11 pt. Goudy OldStyle by FASTpages of Nanuet, NY and printed and bound by Book-mart Press of North Bergen, NJ.

Library of Congress Cataloging-in-Publication Data

Dumas, Didier.
    [Sexualité masculine. English]
    Sons, lovers, and fathers : understanding male sexuality / by
Didier Dumas ; translated and adapted by Anne Trager, Christopher
Fleischner.
       p. cm.
    Includes bibliographical references and index.
    ISBN 0-7657-0033-6 (h/c)
    1. Men—Sexual behavior. 2. Men—Psychology. I. Trager,
Anne. II. Fleischner, Christopher. III. Title.
HQ28.D8613   1996
306.7'081—dc20   96–31300

Printed in the United States of America on acid-free paper. For information and catalog write to Jason Aronson Inc., 230 Livingston Street, Northvale, New Jersey 07647. Or visit our website: http://www.aronson.com

Contents

Contents   vii

Translators' Preface

"Finally a decent book about male sexuality!" we both uttered when we first read Didier Dumas's work, astonished by its ability to restore male dignity. We had discovered a book that painlessly elucidates how men function, demystifying their sexuality, which is so central to their beings as sons, lovers, and fathers, and, as a result, so important to both men and women alike.

Then we noticed our copies disappearing. A friend's teenage son walked off with the first copy. His girlfriend returned it after it had gone through several hands. A colleague complained that his companion filched his copy before he could finish. A middle-aged lawyer and his wife, a doctor, lifted our second copy, our house cleaner the third. "It's that good," we realized, procuring a few more, just in case.

We began to wonder if the enthusiasm exhibited by our French friends would be shared by our American friends. As Americans who have lived in France for many years, we have honed a particular sensitivity to cross-cultural differences. And we both agreed that the news was good enough to spread, that men and women both sides of the Atlantic should be able to benefit from Dumas's insights.

We would like to thank Sheri Holman for encouraging us to pursue our search for a publisher, Janet Petrik for reading through the first draft, Didier Dumas himself for his enthusiastic participation in the adaptation process, all our English-speaking friends for persistently asking when the American version would be ready, and Michael Moskowitz for his enthusiasm for this project.

Anne Trager
Christopher Fleischner
Paris, 1996

Introduction

Women provided the impetus for this book, encouraging me to write it, emphasizing how heavy a burden the roles of wife, mother, and companion become as soon as Adam's desire wavers. At a time when women greatly outdistance men when it comes to talking about their own sexuality, isn't it legitimate to want to do the same?

I shared the idea with those around me, particularly with men. They told me that a book about male sexuality—if it were to be written for them—would have to be stripped of that obscure panoply of concepts usually used by psychotherapists. I argued that this would not be an easy task. "You can't put forth something even slightly new without resorting to an armor of professional vocabulary."

"There you are, right at the heart of the problem," one man laughed. "Do we wear armor when we make love?"

Convinced by this friend, I employ only a few terms from the psychotherapeutic repertoire, and then only familiar ones.

Although the idea originated from women, this book addresses men. It is written by men—by the men who were my patients, whose words I reconstruct, recounting their individual stories as well as the ones they have in common. And it is written for men—for the men of my generation who, like me, had parents who were incapable of answering their questions about sex. Everyone who read the manuscript said, "That's the book I lacked as a teenager." What could I say? Except that this deplorable lack of words about sex led me to become a psychoanalyst.

Although destined for men and women of my age, this book also addresses younger people. It is for my sons, for their cousins, for their friends, for the next generation of men. If it allows sexuality to be something we can talk about from one generation to the next, it will have achieved its goal.

1 The Penis in Erotic Imagination

A woman's role in erection and the extraordinary nature of the penis

"Before I met you," Joe said to me, "I thought what happened when I had sex was entirely up to me. I was always afraid I wouldn't get an erection. Now I believe there are two ways of getting a hard-on: you fantasize, or you feel a woman's desire for you, you feel how she welcomes you. I figured this out last night, and I'll never feel guilty again if I experience impotence."

Joe had spent part of the previous night with a woman he had met a few days earlier. "We were both determined to make love. What a disaster. I didn't understand what came over me. Every time I penetrated her, I lost my erection. We kept trying, though. It was exhausting and I finally left, unsuccessful. On my way home, I felt despondent and ashamed because I hadn't given her the slightest pleasure. Once again, I thought I was impotent. But a surprise awaited me at home: Claudia was in town. I was really happy to see her, but when she started coming on to me, I panicked. I tried to tell her that I couldn't make love, but she wouldn't take no for an answer, and lo and behold I felt an erection coming on. That was a pleasant surprise, considering what had happened earlier. We had no problem making love; I wasn't tired anymore, and it was wonderful. When I woke up, I said to myself that there's no better aphrodisiac than a woman who desires you. The other woman had wanted me, but I don't think she really desired me. That's what made me go so limp."

Two such radically different experiences occurring back to back clearly illustrate to what extent the other's desire influences the quality of sexual pleasure. Above all else, eroticism is a matter of communication. Sexual pleasure would be inconceivable without referring to the other person's desire, which in turn sheds that much more mystery onto the mechanisms which render it possible or impossible, intense or mediocre, satisfying or disappointing. Sexual pleasure involves an emotional encounter, an affinity, a compatibility of fantasies, a harmony between unconscious minds: in short, something totally irrational. Attraction between two people stretches beyond the framework of conscious phenomena. Erotic pleasure delves into the deepest, most personal reaches of the imagination, and the corresponding fantasies bear no semblance of logic. Fantasies may allow minds and bodies to communicate, but not by way of reason, which explains why they are so difficult to understand, if not to accept.

Sex can appear to be a need, one made commercial through prostitution. Yet all cultures consider it an art form not only involving body and mind, but also reaching a spiritual dimension. Sex, like food, is vital. Eating is necessary, but gastronomy transforms the act into an art form by introducing desire, an emotion capable of opening the intellect to spiritual satisfaction. Lovemaking is also art. Sexual pleasure may involve the body, but if limited to the body alone it becomes a source of dissatisfaction. The void created by an orgasm bereft of words and feelings can transform a sexual encounter into an experience as intolerable as it is intense. Sensual pleasure, however remarkable, only brings peace of mind when emotionally satisfying.

Mankind differs from other animal species in that our sexuality is not governed by seasonal cycles, but by our own desire, which leads to the first difficulty we encounter as sexual beings: we must make up our own minds about our sexuality. We can use it to perpetuate the human race, or we can use it exclusively for pleasure. Here we pinpoint a feature of our status as humans: we stand as the sole judges of the validity of our own desires, fantasies, and acts. This explains why sexual pleasure can be frightening. Animals did not invent family planning, nor did they invent concentration camps. Fear of our own fantasies thus remains a legitimate fear for mankind.

Despite the complex bonds between sexuality and desire, we still have a tendency to consider male sexual pleasure as straightforward. If a man is not impotent, he is supposed to be satisfied by the orgasm of ejaculation. Compared to the veils that shroud female sexuality, we reduce male sexuality to something trite and empty of mystery. We strip it down to a crude biological function that obeys only the dictates of nature. We complaisantly associate virility with all tolerable forms of brutality and, by the same token, relegate it to the arena of those "springtime" yearnings that lose their cutting edge with age.

However—and quite to the contrary—our culture's religious and mythological framework represents male sexuality as out of the ordinary, endowed with a mystery of its own. The manner in which Zeus appears as a bird or as a shower of golden rain from one coitus to another raises as many questions as the manner in which the Christian God presents himself to the Virgin Mary by way of an angel. Language also seems to consider erection as unusual and even startling in its mystery. Most languages reveal an astonishing wealth of terms for the male sexual organ in action. Richard A. Spears's *Slang and Euphemism* numbers over three hundred terms for penis in the English language.

This sheer verbal proliferation endows the male organ with a unique status in spoken language. Has any other single object produced such an exuberant burgeoning of terms and images, which may not crop up in everyday use but which hold a definite place in the language?

The *membrum virile* gives rise to an explosion of representations, which can be classified into a relatively limited number of groups. Among the most prolific metaphors are objects that evoke the shape of the penis: *shaft, hose, staff, pole,* or *joystick.* Linked to one or another of its functions, the shape becomes a *wedge, prick,* or *probe* that penetrates; a *wick, pipe,* or *bonfire* that burns with the fires of desire; a *root* that gives life or a *gardener* that sows seed.

Other terms refer to the position the penis occupies in the fantasies of both sexes. Food metaphors abound: *banana, cream stick, kosher pickle, live sausage, carrot,* and *cucumber*—to name only a few—all evoke the organ's relationship to the vaginal mouth it is supposed to feed. Weapons form another category: *blade, trigger, sword, dagger, gun,* and *bayonet* all embody the exaltation of a virility sharpened by combat and by the absence of women on the battlefield. Another category equates the penis with musical instruments—*bugle, flute, drumstick, trombone, fiddle bow*—associating the vibrations of sexual pleasure with musical resonance.

Other expressions designate the male organ as an asset reflecting status, authority, or control over destiny. It becomes an *affair,* one's *pride and joy,* a *master of ceremonies,* a *family organ,* a *sceptre,* or a *magic wand.* When referred to as *Saint Peter, Abraham, Old Adam,* or *father confessor,* it becomes sacred and clothed with a personality, which brings us to a final category of images representing the penis: those that identify it with a living being—an animal or a person—or to that being's psychological qualities. Among the animals, we encounter the *cock, stallion, eel, one-eyed worm,* or *dragon. Uncle Dick, Peter, little brother,* and *man Thomas* identify the penis with a person, while *mad mick, stormy dick, old horny,* and *Julius Caesar* depict it as a psychological type complete with dominant character traits.

This last category highlights a difference between male and female sexuality. Unlike women, men do not experience their sexual organs as being one with their bodies. Very early in life, a boy must confront the autonomy of his penis. He does not control his erections; they can arise unexpectedly, and he perceives his penis as a little person with whom he must come to terms. When he has an erection independently of his will, he relinquishes his position at the center of his being to this sexual organ that expresses itself on its own. Two possible solutions exist: he either complies with his penis, or he silences it. And this little appendage's independence can at times create discomfort: a boy suffering from untimely erections will not find the situation very agreeable. Therefore, the dialogue a man establishes with his penis is of the utmost importance, for it holds the keys to harmony between his heart and his groin, between his feelings and his sexual impulses.

Dreams provide fertile ground for demonstrations of the male member's autonomy. Men suffering from obsessional neurosis[1] often dream that their penises separate from their bodies and fly through the air, providing oneiric compensation for the pathological immobility generated by this neurosis. In other dreams, men will represent their penises as vehicles, motorcycles, horses, or any other means of locomotion that enables them to exhibit courage and daring. No less frequent are dreams in which they represent their penises as animals gifted with phenomenal abilities. Let's examine a dream from one of my French patients who suffered from sexual inhibition.

---

1. Obsession and hysteria are two major forms of neurosis and causes of sexual inhibition.

"I was in bed in the house we lived in when I was a kid, and my mother was in the room next door. All of the sudden, I felt a strange animal under the sheets attached to my body by a leash. I'd never seen an animal like that before: half mammal, half bird. It was a kind of peacock (paon in French, pronounced "pā") with the head of a stag (cerf in French, pronounced "sɛr"). I wasn't afraid, instead I was really excited about the idea of showing my mother this fantastic animal. I unleashed the creature with my hands so it could go to my mother, but it immediately evaporated, making me very sad. Then I saw stains on the sheets and I couldn't tell what colour they were. I wondered if they were red or white, unable to decide between the two."

This dream illustrates how the child this dreamer once was imagined his own sexual organ. In French this animal would be called a *cerf-paon*, pronounced [sɛrpā], which sounds exactly like the French word *serpent*, meaning snake. Yet despite the fact that the *cerf-paon* could be construed as a snake, it was, in fact, a cross between a stag and a peacock, and not a snake.

Rarely does a man represent his penis as a snake. Out of the three hundred odd terms for the penis listed by Spears, snake or snake-related words appear only four times, generally in reference to length or the ability to be charmed. It is primarily in women's imagination that the snake evokes the penis, because it symbolizes the role that femininity plays in arousing the male sexual organ.

In all mythologies, this animal that glides over the ground symbolizes earth energy, and consequently femininity. In the Judeo-Christian Genesis myth, the serpent represents how Eve tempted Adam to commit the sin of the flesh, and has no particular relationship to Adam himself; instead, it symbolizes the woman's tools of seduction: her own energies that breathe life into the male organ. The Judeo-Christian myth thus presents the mystery of phallicity as a direct consequence of female desire. The quality of an erection is, in fact, proportional to the receptivity of the vagina that arouses it and, in erotic imagery, the snake always represents the female forces that give strength to erection.

A man, however, would find it hard to confuse his penis with an animal condemned to sliding over the ground because the penis's nature lifts it skyward. For this reason, it has been called *bird*, *skyscraper*, and *star gazer*. A boy can only imagine his penis as a snake when it appears to be sleeping. This particular sleeper's desire substituted a stag and a peacock for the snake, since both animals bear celestial qualities. The peacock's fanned tail and the size of the horns that crown the stag's head far more appropriately evoke the pride he takes in his erections.

As a child, the dreamer had wanted his mother to admire this pride. The hands that unleash the creature suggest masturbation. The volatility of the animal represents detumescence, and the white or red spots earmark a question concerning sexual maturity. Do boys make red stains similar to menstruation or white stains? Another man would have dreamed another creature attached to his body with other associations, depending on his own unconscious perplexities.

A taboo concerning precisely these questions had reigned during my patient's childhood. His mother, like far too many mothers, had become totally oblivious to her femininity when she entered maternity. An excellent mother, she nevertheless hampered her son's sexual development by forbidding any talk about sex. In this case, answering her son's questions about his anatomy did not profoundly disturb this mother; rather, she feared letting him perceive her own pleasure or disgust in arousing a penis. As a result, she forbade any talk about her own femininity.

Consequently, the child couldn't make any sense of his erections. In his relationship to his mother, the child could not show pride in his sexual organ and, as an adult, he suffered from sexual inhibition. The *cerf-paon* dream tried to express this dilemma. Like a childhood puzzle, he used an invisible snake to represent his mother's invisible femininity which he rediscovered through an aggregation of two male animals that, like father and son, manifest very visible phallic assets.

The role of the unconscious in sexuality

Sexual pleasure can feel like a prodigious energy vibrating throughout the body, providing a potential for ecstasy. Yet as soon as we ask questions about the sources of our pleasure, all logic disappears. Some men get turned on by big breasts, others little ones, others high heels as seen in certain forms of fetishism. The same applies to the body's erogenous zones. The penis is not necessarily the only erogenous zone on the male body. For some men, the tip of the nipple produces extreme pleasure, for others, the anus, regardless of homosexual or heterosexual orientation. For both men and women, the body parts that concentrate sexual arousal invariably differ from one subject to another, just as they resonate at varying degrees of intensity. One of the first stumbling blocks we encounter when we ask questions in this area resides in sexual pleasure's defiance of the normal references set by rational, logical thought.

Like food, sexuality rebalances body energy. Yet sexual difficulties stem not so much from the body and the need, but more often from desire and psychic communication. Of course, sexual pleasure resonates in the body, but it nevertheless depends upon its governing fantasies. It does not simply correspond to a physical need because it involves, above all, an ability to come to terms with the complexity of one's own desire and inner fantasy life. As a result, sexual love is a highly personal art form. The ability to take one's own idiosyncracies and imagination seriously, the pleasure of making dreams come true and sharing them with a partner through sex, transform eroticism into a very private art. More difficult to exchange than the culinary arts shared around a table, we practice eroticism only in the strictest intimacy, which accounts for the difficulty we having putting words to our experiences.

Talking about sexual pleasure implies admitting that the unconscious mind plays a larger role in this domain than the conscious mind. The conscious mind governs the immediate survival of the person, while the unconscious mind reaches much further: it governs the survival of the species. It therefore inevitably works its way into eroticism. *Sexual pleasure springs from unconscious communication between psyches; it bypasses the use of words, and for this reason harbors frailty and mystery.* Any potential difficulties lie in the fact that unconscious minds are communicating.

Erotic communication brings desire into play, rendering it satisfying or disappointing. Different from needs that require actual physical satisfaction, desire can be fulfilled on a nonmaterial level. A nonsexual encounter can be just as much an expression of desire as a sexual one. Love can be platonic and desire aimed at God, or dependent upon a whole variety of nonmaterial objects that populate our thoughts and imagination, making it easy for desire to mistake its choice of object. The same applies to erotic communication, which depends upon a meeting of fantasies that themselves tell only part of the story behind the unconscious encounter required for bodily pleasure. Therefore, despite all our efforts, outlining what intensifies pleasure to ecstasy with certain partners remains as difficult as understanding what renders it persistently bland with others. Satisfying or disappointing, sexual pleasure appears to be unaware of its own driving forces. Erotic communication eludes the conscious process: it is the relationship between one unconscious mind and another that determines mutual attraction and creates the force of eroticism.

We have now pinpointed the main reason people have difficulty talking about their sexuality. Of course, a person can be perfectly aware of the specifics of his or her own fantasies, but as long as that person doesn't make sense of them in relation to another person his or her fantasies retain every appearance of being a mental counterpart to masturbation. On the other hand, as soon as we make love, fantasies cease to weigh us down, and the pleasures of erotic communication rid us of all need to verbalize our fantasies.

The possibility of talking about sexual intimacy appeared rather recently in our culture. It dates from the beginning of the century and is one of psychoanalysis's undeniable contributions to Western thought. The evolution of language bears witness to this change. The verb *fantasize*—and what we have come to understand by it—does not even appear in dictionaries prior to the development of psychoanalysis. The first recorded use of the verb *fantasize* dates from 1926 with the loose meaning "of representing in the fancy." Only later does the verb take on the meaning that derives from psychoanalysis. *Fantasy* has a far longer pedigree, stretching back to the fourteenth century. As a noun, it first referred to the use of the imagination, later to an apparition or a phantom, whereas as a verb it meant to fancy or to imagine. Only in 1926 do we find an example—specific to psychoanalysis—of its use with the meaning we now ascribe to it.

Through this linguistic evolution, we can observe the decisive step taken by our culture in terms of sexuality. That the word fantasy developed little by little into an active verb indicates the new importance that the twentieth century attributes to the faculties of imagination, both in sexuality and in creativity in general.

The quality of erotic pleasure does not depend on conscious verbal communication; it depends on fantasies, on an interplay between unconscious minds, from which stem the strangeness and fragility of this pleasure. That the twentieth century views sexuality in a new light therefore results as much from the new tools for conceptualizing sexuality provided by psychoanalysis as it does from the development of contraception.

Since sexuality relies much more on unconscious rather than conscious communication, we do not necessarily find it easy to talk about it with our lovers. Paradoxically, it is far easier to talk about it in a relationship that excludes bodily contact, such as the one that serves as the basis of all forms of psychotherapy: a relationship in which there is no place for erotic exchanges, but in which we can speak about everything that concerns sex.

In this way, psychoanalysts—and psychotherapists—take on the role that once belonged to confessors and exorcists. Of course, the former do not dispense moral authority, which is the novelty of their role. They allow people to delve into their own sexuality and lives. They assume the mantle of priesthood only insofar as they deal with pathologies of the psyche.

Psychoanalysis explores the formation of the mind and tries to understand human mental development, and—with psychotherapy—is one of the few practices that recognises the need to cry. People consult psychotherapists about problems they have with themselves, in their relationships with their partners, their parents, their children, or other people in general. Above all, the therapist's role is to provide a place for testimony. People talk to their therapists about their sexuality as they would to nobody else. At the same time, patients teach their therapists useful information worth sharing. So the therapeutic profession consists partly in listening to patients and partly in making sense of and making known what we learn.

What men teach us about their sexuality

In the following two chapters, we will examine how sexual fantasies are formed in childhood and how Freud understood the male child's sexual development. Although Freud rightly points out that sexual fantasies are formed in childhood through the child's relationship to his parents or parent substitutes, this process depends as much on the parents' unconscious minds as it does on their conscious minds. Beginning in adolescence, a person's sexual fantasies can be either interfered with or activated by a whole coven of phantoms that spring directly from the parents' unconscious minds. This is generally what lies at the root of what is known as sexual perversion. In these cases, sexuality takes on a whole range of bizarre forms with apparently only one goal: to exorcise an unconscious issue inherited from the parents.

Etymologically, perverted means "turned the wrong way around." Perverse sexuality remains turned towards the parents, instead of being invested in future adulthood and in procreation. Unlike neurotics who suffer sexual inhibition, perverts are particularly inventive in their sexuality. In its approach to sexual perversion, Freudian theory remains insufficient because it neglects to recognize that the parents' neuroses—or more simply, the fact that they may themselves actually have an unconscious mind—could in any way influence the child's development and the elaboration of his sexual fantasies. I do not want to weigh down this book with a theoretical discussion that I have already treated elsewhere (Dumas 1985, 1989). Instead, I have simply chosen to present two cases of perversion that, in a certain respect, speak for themselves.

The first case study, about an inveterate Don Juan, reveals the mechanisms of a certain kind of male sexuality in which a man seems to be unable to do anything other than hop from one partner to another. We will see how this man discovered the strange role played by the compulsive nature of his sexuality: it guarded the secret of his father's impotence.

The second, about a rubber fetishist, contradicts the Freudian point of view. We know that Freud viewed sexual fetishes as substitutes for an imaginary penis that the male child attributes to his mother. Freud had different reasons for drawing this conclusion, among which was the fact that fetishism is a sexual disturbance that seems to affect only men. The case that I present provides an entirely different explanation of why fetishism is, above all, a masculine perversion. This man's need to call on a fetish in order to attain orgasm did not stem from a difficulty conceptualizing that a mother does not have a penis. He was raised by an obsessional mother who, concerned about the elasticity of his foreskin, regularly masturbated him on a rubber apron. This man thus suffered due to a precocious seduction that he had never been able to name as such. Unable, at that age, to conceive of his mother as incestuous, the child attributed the pleasure he experienced with his mother to the presence of the rubber apron. Yet, although his fixation could be traced to his childhood experience, his mother was not solely responsible. The words his father chose to speak to him, at that age, about sexuality played a central role, rendering idealization of the male sexual organ definitively impossible. We shall see how this sexual passion for rubber hid this man's ineffable grief at not being born a girl.

By reducing everything to the fear of discovering the mother's gaping sex, Freudian theory totally neglects the role the testicles play in the development of male sexuality. I have therefore dedicated an entire chapter to the subject. Freudian theory also neglects the role that fantasies associating virility and the arts of war play in phallic eroticism. Yet manhood has always been associated with the arts of war: phallic sexuality feeds on warrior fantasies, expressed as much through the erotic experience of virility as through the social expressions of masculinity and political power. In the chapter that I have devoted to the subject, I will demonstrate how the homosexual element of warrior fantasies places a premium on manhood and, as a result, reaches the same depth of meaning in erotic pleasure for both sexes.

Adulthood is the age at which our parents become old, the age at which we rule, replacing the former generation and becoming reigning figures for the generation to come. Adult men and women both must face the loss of the bodily dimensions of the relationship to their own mothers, and they do so differently. Women reconstruct it in their relationship to their own children, whereas men join other men of their own age in groups, clubs, parties, teams, churches, or armies. Groups of friends play a mothering role during adolescence, substituting for the mother's body in order to create space for their own generation. At this stage, mixed peer groups are still tolerated. But as soon as the group ceases to be mixed, becoming a group of men, and one member raises his head above the others, becoming a leader, as soon as it takes shape in the form of a party, a church, or an athletic team, it no longer substitutes for the mother's body, but for the father's.

Be he destined for the military or priesthood, for politics or meditation, for economics or the quest for knowledge, the social expression of a man's sexuality bears the imprint of a father's hidden presence. Organized religion and the military form the two prime models for all male institutions. A man uses a double model to reconstruct the lost relationship with the father's body: he either reaches towards heaven, choosing priesthood and becoming a father without having to pass through any other mother except the one on the pediment of his church; or he chooses arms, economics, or politics, which means he reconstructs his father's body on an earthly level, identifying with the nation's borders. Whatever his choice, his relationship to erotic pleasure is nevertheless dependent upon the relationship that, as a child, bound him to his mother.

We will discover in these pages how the Maternal—all that which relates to the mother—profoundly determines the unconscious desire that animates male sexuality. Listen to men on a daily basis talk about themselves and their sexuality and a predominate topic emerges: Mother. For she is far more present than Woman. Of course, men talk a lot about women, but when these women create problems, it is rarely as women and more often as mothers.

Femininity, the necessary complement to virility, has no reason in and of itself to be offensive to masculinity. On the contrary, it triggers its expansion. Therefore, by nature, men tend to be indulgent with all that touches on femininity, with the Feminine, while images of the Maternal remain more problematic for them. When a man talks about a woman—she may be a mother, or want to become one; she may or may not remind him of his own mother—his attraction or aversion to that woman will always, consciously or unconsciously, make reference to his own mother.

With Freud, we began to understand that the unconscious desire that arouses male sexuality takes root in the relationship with the mother. Fewer questions have been asked about the opposing duality of Maternal and Feminine images in male imagination. For men, a woman is either mother or partner in pleasure, but rarely the two at once. His sexual fantasies never superimpose Mother and Woman. Images of femininity sharpen his sexual desires; those of maternity are more likely to inhibit it.

The same applies to women. In their sexual and libidinal balance, maternity and femininity oppose each other like opposite ends on a scale of values. Feeling torn between husband and children is a major theme among women. Numerous women observe that a child's arrival turns them away from their spouses, weighing heavily on their femininity. Certain women, like the mother of the man who dreamed of the *cerf-paon*, renounce femininity when they become mothers, locking themselves into a neurosis that, in turn, inhibits their children's sexual development.

The ease with which religions, which are primarily male institutions, oppose the immaculate mother and the whore clearly sums up a difficulty inherent in male desire. For a mother to play a central role in a male child's sexual development, he must be able to view her as a woman replete with a sexuality of her own and a relationship with men. A boy will perceive his mother as a woman through the eyes of an adult male— those of his father or father substitute—and thus be ousted from the position in which he first viewed her as a mother. Male imagination therefore always casts a double image of women. If he views her as a woman, he places himself in continuity with his father, while if he views her as a mother, he places himself in continuity with the child, occupying a position next to his mother that he has since left vacant.

Femininity associates sex with enjoyment and pure sexual pleasure. Maternity refers sex to a succession of generations and to death. *Sexual desire expresses itself fully in its struggle between two opposing planes. One—horizontal—places sex in its relationship to pleasure and the space of one's own generation.* This plane encompasses the images of witch and whore that occupy male fantasies, both holding the keys to pleasure. *The other—vertical—places sex in relationship to a succession of generations, to time, to reproduction and to death.* This plane produces the images of maternity that, in male imagination, guarantee the way in which a man assumes paternity.

The act of turning away from the mother, however, is a statement of virility. A man's relationship to his own mother can continue to determine his sexual dynamics throughout his life. For him, as for his partner, eroticism remains the burial ground for the first object of his love, yet, although a man's words about his sexuality are polarized on the mother, he is not always referring to his own mother. The maternal image's grasp on men's expression results from the duty incumbent on manliness: re-creating a mother. Whether we accept it or refuse it, is that not the goal of every ejaculation? That man creates and supports maternity implies for him the necessity of knowing how to oppose it, if only to be able to freely assume its responsibility.

Male unconscious desire is therefore always ambivalent when faced with the mother. Ejaculation's mini-birth can hardly rival the phallicity of the maternal belly that gives birth, so manhood tends to turn away from the mother. Its characteristic actions run counter to motherhood, such as when it glorifies combat and the arts of war and, in doing so, only antagonistically accepts its complementary role. Where motherhood assumes the responsibility of maintaining life, manhood undertakes and regulates the existence of death. In his own way, a priest will do the same, and in this respect, Christ was not lacking in virility. "Woman, what have I to do with thee?" he said to his mother, Mary; he also said, "I must be about my father's business."

In every tradition, war and religion oppose and complement the Maternal. This world's civilizations flourish in their very diversity, yet they all share one common denominator: excluding from war and religious activities not necessarily all women, but those women who are mothers or destined to become mothers. History provides no examples of women who take up arms or prophecy during maternity. There are two women prophets in the Bible, but they are warriors like Joan of Arc who, in a manly fashion, renounced maternity.

Soldier and priest are two male activities that radically oppose motherhood, precisely because mothers are excluded. For a man to be able to think of himself as a man, he must have pulled himself away from a mother. Virility's conscious or unconscious goals unavoidably focus on the relationship to the Maternal, and therefore determine whether one accepts or refuses the consequences of manhood. But whether he opposes the Maternal or gives himself the charge of perpetuating it, the unconscious desire that animates male sexuality never expresses itself in a direct relationship with a man's own mother, but rather in the strange language of fantasies that inspire his sexual being.

Although his mother is central to his sexual development, a man would find it difficult to have sexual fantasies with direct representations of the woman who brought him into the world. The role of erotic fantasies is to open his mind to the landscapes of adult sexuality, while excluding infantile visions that would evoke his mother. One person cannot exchange his fantasies for another's. They correspond to something deeply rooted in the unconscious mind, beyond that person's power to simply change them, thus indicating that they originate in childhood, when the foundations of a person's sexuality are cast. His fantasies must nevertheless banish all infantile visions of himself in order to play their role in adult sexuality. Sexual fantasies correspond to a language that is used only in eroticism. They establish a bridge between the unconscious that governs sex and the conscious that is accountable for one's acts. Since the dialect of fantasies opposes—or complements—logical thought and the faculties of judgment, let us now explore the intricacies of this language, the language of eroticism.

2 How Fantasies Arouse Sexual Desire

The early discovery of sexuality and the formation of fantasies

A teenage boy perceives his growing sexual mobility through the changing responses he experiences in his relationships, notably with the other sex. Some people become more attractive than others, eliciting an emotion that activates the imagination and eroticizes the body. Sexuality's awakening manifests itself through a variety of signals and images that stir the genitalia: perhaps shapely curves or smooth skin, a scent or a voice, hair color or glistening eyes—all signals that seem to promise the pleasure expected from a sexual encounter.

During this same period, we become aware of our sexual fantasies. Fantasies play a primary role in sexual arousal and the promise of pleasure that follows. And just like erogenous zones, everybody has their own collection of images and representations that signal sexual desire and resonate in the body to differing degrees.

Sexual fantasies serve to maintain the vitality of those images and representations that allow us to rediscover the initial revelation that sexual pleasure was for us. They govern sexual functioning and are accomplice to the intensity of pleasure that accompanies love-making. Among other things, they are essential to masturbation. When men report the personal details of their masturbation fantasies, a majority describe them using images of women with whom they experienced particularly pleasurable sex, and when their fantasies revolve around a specific woman, she is generally the first woman with whom that man experienced sexual pleasure as a revelation. She is not necessarily the first woman he knew, but rather the woman with whom erotic play revealed a quality and intensity of pleasure never before experienced.

A smaller number of men understand and explain their fantasies according to a childhood revelation, which is the case when, as children, they had been sexually seduced by an adult. Such an event represents a revelation permanently engraved in their fantasies.

The discovery of sexual pleasure can occur early in life. Capable of experiencing orgasm long before reaching maturity, a child, in any case, feels oral and anal pleasure, just as he can encounter genital pleasure precociously, since a boy does not depend on mature testicles in order to become wise to his penis and its role in pleasure. At a young age, boys can experience dry orgasms similar to those of men who have had prostate operations. Yet this discovery can take different forms. Let's now look at two opposing examples of how a boy can encounter sensual pleasure.

Bill's fantasies concentrated on older women, something he owed to his nanny. When he was 4 or 5 years old, a cleaning women came to take care of him at home. She must have been 40 or 50 years old. "In one of my earliest memories, I see her taking my penis into her mouth after my bath and sucking on it gently.

It gave me fabulous shivers. I remember it well. She always asked me if I liked it. I continued to have oral relations with her until the age of 9 or 10, when my mother stopped working and dismissed this woman. I generally fantasize about women who are around 60 years old—the older the better. They have to have experience, and I imagine them trembling and moaning like my nanny did. Even now, I'm perfectly happy making love exclusively with older women."

Bill's attraction to mature women did not generate problems for him and was not the reason he came to see me. As a matter of fact, he introduced this episode as "the childhood secret that gave me self-confidence." Now let's look at an opposite case.

"Even though I became a pretty well-known actor," Steve said to me during our first appointment, "I never felt at ease with my sexuality." His parents were very young when he was born, and his mother died shortly after his birth. He had the impression that his father never forgave him for her death, which was his way of explaining the difficult relationship he had with his father. Unable to take care of his son, his father abandoned himself to a life of debauchery, addressing his son only to mistreat him. Women kept coming and going, and that is how Steve discovered sexuality.

"One day, one of these women came on to me, probably as a joke. I must have been around 10. My father was out. She sat on the bed, took my hand and drew me closer. She caressed me near my penis. I got a hard-on, and I remember that she thought it was very funny. She took out my penis, bent over, touched it with her lips and began to suck. I thought my head was going to explode. I didn't know what to do with the feelings that came over me. Right at that moment, my father came home. The woman said I had come on to her and she had only wanted to make me happy. My father became violent. He knocked me about and threatened to cut off my penis. For a long time, I was terrorized by the idea that he might carry out his threat.

"At the time, I didn't understand her intentions. I was excited, but I didn't understand what she was doing. Now I know that she used me as a toy, and that must have marked me. I've always been afraid of women. Before I got married, I was never able to go all the way with a woman. I was full of anxiety, afraid that she was only using me for her own pleasure. This fear came back in my fantasies. I would see myself with my father's friend, trying to seduce her without her mocking me. Even now, I feel fragile in my manhood. In my business, I meet a lot of women who come on to me. I tend to run away from them because I'm always afraid they're only interested in me as an object. It's as if I saw them all in the image of my father's friend."

These two examples reveal that the early discovery of sexuality can color sexual fantasies for a lifetime. They also clarify how sexual relations between children and adults can be traumatic. If the adult who seduces a child addresses him with respect for his desires and his person, the experience is rarely referred to as traumatic. On the contrary, if the child had his body and his desire violated by an adult who treated him as an object, it is rare for that person as an adult to forgive his aggressor. Physical pain is easily forgotten, but emotional pain is another story. Memories cannot be erased that easily. Being treated like a disposable plaything is always destructive. When an experience of this kind coincides with the revelation of sexual pleasure, it is particularly difficult to forget. Sexual fantasies depend on the first experiences that reveal the intensity of sexual pleasure. Using these events as building blocks, fantasies integrate and nourish traumatic memories that adult eroticism may have difficulty surmounting.

The trauma lies not in having been sexually seduced by an adult in and of itself, but rather in, on this occasion, having integrated the concept of a sexuality disconnected from the emotional processes that account for the quality of communication between people.

The most common hindrance that an adult imposes on a child's sexual development usually stems, on the contrary, from the fear of considering the child as a sexual object. Parents perceive their child as an asexual being in order to protect themselves from their own fear of incest. At the same time, they keep the child from being able to fantasize himself in the role and the seduction that are proper to his own sexuality. Here, the child also integrates a conception of sexuality that is disconnected from emotions and is therefore traumatic.

At a time when we are only beginning to recognize children's sexuality, the infantile trauma experienced by the majority of psychotherapy patients lies primarily in the impossibility they had, as children, of integrating a coherent concept of sexuality. An adult's fantasies appear completely disconnected from the emotional processes primarily because the child was unable to imagine and understand his parents' sexual mechanisms. Therefore, fantasies cause fear. In solitude or masturbation, the incomprehensible crudeness of sexual fantasies can only give rise to problems.

The mechanisms involved in erotic seduction

Fantasies also turn up in the initial encounter with a sexual partner, although not expressed in the same manner. What happens when a man meets a woman he doesn't know but finds attractive? First of all, an image—a certain number of signals—catches his attention. The signals given off by the other person trigger erotic attraction, but the indicators that allow a man to perceive an unknown woman as a possible sexual partner stem primarily from his own erotic sensibility, thus providing him only with information about his own fantasies.

Sexual attraction takes advantage of the desired person's qualities, but not in a rational manner, precisely because it is activated by fantasies. Imagination can amplify the qualities attributed to the other person, just as it can invent other qualities. Fantasies twist and deny reality in order to attain their goals. The heart has its reasons which reason knows nothing of, and what makes another person sexually attractive to us does not necessarily tell us about the real, objective qualities of that person. It only enlightens us about ourselves and our own fantasies. Erotic images appear to emanate from those who attract us but, in fact, they emerge from an unfolding of our own fantasy-related sensibility. Eroticism thus goes hand in hand with the ability to project onto the other person, if not one's own crude fantasies, at least a certain number of images that enable sexual arousal.

Seen from this angle, sexual desire is, above all, a phenomenon of projection. Reinforced by the power of fantasies, imagination is not exempt from traps. The real man never coincides with the Prince Charming who occupies the little girl's dreams, and the divine appearances endowed upon a man's mistress enable him to avoid confronting the reality of that woman's real intentions. This is one of the characteristics of human sexuality. Adult sexuality remains in continuity with the child's sexuality: a child sees his parents as flesh-and-blood divinities; an adult man is just as capable of projecting onto a woman the goddess who holds the keys to his soul.

Fantasies: thoughts as images

The fantasy projection that inspires sexual arousal makes preferential use of images. Ordinary thought processes favor reason and words; erotic thought gives priority to images. Linked to one another in a scenario, erotic images form a mental sexual fuel. Certain images will have a greater effect than others in activating the fantasy motor, which explains the proliferation of pornographic magazines and films: by commercializing images to provoke erections, to a certain extent they allow a person to accelerate the erotic motor while remaining in neutral, that is, in absence of communication with another person.

Everybody possesses imaginative fantasies of their own. Pornography's banal uniformity testifies to the impossibility that human beings have in eliminating their fantasies. The conscious mind and the faculty of reason have little hold over the omnipresence of fantasy-related images. The unconscious force of sexual fantasies easily overturns all the barriers that the moral, conscious mind tries to construct, for it is ruled by words, while the unconscious flourishes with images that—like dreams—elude the normal order of thoughts. Everyone feels bizarre fantasies arising from the unconscious, revealing themselves as scenarios. "Don't make a scene," a man will say to somebody who is hassling him, whereas if he is open to a woman's charms, he won't see if she "was putting on a show."

Thus, for adults, sexual fantasies impose themselves on the mind like a succession of images that are not only personal, but also relatively static—they come back time and time again in an identical form. In the example of masturbation, the succession of images is as essential to pleasure as the work of the hand. The monotony and poverty of imaginary scenarios used for masturbatory arousal accounts for the discomfort often experienced. The scenario can, of course, vary, but as it unfolds the subject nevertheless repeats itself unchanged. This repetitive expression testifies to a lack of erotic communication. Could masturbation really compensate for anything else? Fantasies express a need for sexual communication. In order to do so, they highlight memories of previous erotic experiences, including childhood experiences.

From this perspective, masturbation fantasies can appear rather paltry. One finds basic representations of coitus, or images that are otherwise cruder, even in the eyes of the person who produces them. The former can vibrate with an emotion rooted in the depths of the being, while the latter present the penis in its relationship to all the other bodily orifices: the vagina, but also the anus, the mouth, the breasts, the eyes, or the nostrils. Be they fantasies that revolve around such frightening and fascinating things as sadomasochism or around other erotic behaviors, their primary characteristic is an ability to appear as incredible as they are incomprehensible to the person who uses them for his or her own pleasure.

When they appear contrary to one's moral standings or one's conscience, such a production of images can be experienced as burdensome. There are no words to talk about it. Shame and guilt barricade an enclosure where the fantasy lives on like a devil that, because inside, creates a feeling of being double. Thus, in his own fantasies, the respectable Dr. Jekyll becomes the terrible Mr. Hyde, whom he embodies when the night falls. The major problem lies in the person's inability to understand his or her own language of fantasy. Fantasies are nothing more than thoughts transformed into images. Yet one still has to understand the logic of this strange dialect upon which sexuality depends.

The role of the other's pleasure in fantasies

Although they may appear burdensome, fantasies support and serve as a motor in adult male sexuality—which is their primary function and, by the same token, makes them necessary. Experienced as the chuckling of an inner devil, they are actually nothing more than the reminder of a vital function: the necessity of experiencing one's sexuality that accompanies adulthood. Fantasies are formed during childhood, but what does the child's fantasizing process correspond to?

Imagine a 4- or 5-year-old child who wants to play with his mother. He asks her, and she says it's impossible, she has other things to do. Faced with his mother, he understands the rationality of the argument and goes off to play alone in his room. But in solitude, while playing, he reinterprets the event that impeded his desire: the fantasizing process sets to work. In a dialogue with imaginary people, he makes them understand that his mother's obligation to do something else deprived her of the very great pleasure of playing with him. If he experienced his mother's refusal as a punishment, he could even reprocess the event, explaining that he necessarily deprived his mother of the pleasure that she would have had if he had let her play with him. We see the work of fantasies. *Fantasies return the subject to an active position in situations where the fulfilment of his desire depends on somebody else.* With his rational thought processes, the child can understand that his mother has something other to do than play with him, but in his fantasies he seems to be ignorant of the fact that she could be governed by something other than his own desire.

A child who is abused by his parents provides another example: in his rational thought processes, the child can conceive of the punishment as one he deserves. But if the event is repeated too many times, he will tend to interpret it, in his fantasies, as an undeniable sign of the irresistible desire that his parents have for him. He may then develop masochistic fantasies in order to not deprive them of the pleasure he gives them. Seen from this angle, we begin to understand why sadomasochistic eroticism appears so frequently among adults.

In adult sexuality, erotic fantasies sustain the same mechanisms that gave them form during childhood. They can thus act out events that, in daily life, would be experienced as very disagreeable. The idea of hitting someone or of being hit, the idea of surprising someone in his nudity or having one's intimacy violated can all rank equally on a scale of erotic arousal. Masochistic fantasies focus on creating an all-powerful master in matters of sexuality. Sadistic fantasies attempt to enhance the value of the other's pleasure. Voyeuristic fantasies strive to capture the other's pleasure. Exhibitionist fantasies try to provoke it.

Sexual fantasies are representations that appear as party to another's pleasure. The pleasure they provoke or precede affirms the possibility of placing oneself in the leading role in this pleasure. The manner in which they express themselves as active or passive is independent of the subject's gender. In fantasies, it is primarily the "I" responsible for desire that ascribes itself the central role in the other's pleasure. "I want to see" or "I want to be seen," "I want to hit" or "I want to be hit" are propositions that, with equal intensity, enable a person to stand on one or the other side of a duality of pleasure.

Fantasies can shock or displease. They can even make undesirable intrusions in the mind. Yet they are nevertheless the product of a process of mental maturation that took place during childhood. That they are sexual changes nothing in the fact that imagination is dependent upon a system of representations that is only integrated after birth. Therefore, *erotic fantasies are the product of the manner in which the child developed his mind in the area of sexual exploration.*

Don Juan and his father's ghost[1]

A person's fantasy life is not limited to his sexual fantasies, which are only one source signaling the unconscious roots of the fantasizing process. On this level, psychotherapy is one of the only paths in our culture that has attempted to understand something about the unconscious mind and the fantasies through which it is expressed. The work is sometimes arduous. Sexual fantasies take root in early childhood, formed in relationship with the parents' conscious minds—with what the parents say—and also in relationship with their unconscious minds—with what the parents silence. Certain bizarre aspects of sexual scenarios do not only concern the childhood and the individual story of the person who produces them. They can hide a traumatic childhood situation that adulthood tries in vain to forget, just as they can stem from a parent's story, or even a grandparent's. They can be the product

---

1. This case study as well as the following one were already published in *Le Bloc-notes de la psychanalyse*, number 9 (Geneva: Georg Editeur, 1990).

of what we inherit from our ancestors. In this case, the metaphor of fantasies as fuel in adult sexuality remains valid, but the sexuality vehicle—which is ruled by its own laws—seems to be driven by a ghost. The perpetual Don Juan often provides a good illustration of this phenomenon.

What is this strange voyage that leads Don Juan to the obligation of satisfying all the women who pass his way? Doesn't the infernal rhythm of this kind of sexuality evoke a journey to a land of ghosts?

One of my patients had developed this kind of sexuality and, from what he said, didn't seem to get any rest at all between his erotic frolicking. While very young, this Don Juan deflowered a very impressive number of cousins, thus gaining a foothold in the world of women and in the passion of unraveling their mysteries. He developed the capacity of maintaining five or six more or less stable relationships at one time, which did not keep him from burning with an ardent desire for the next female figure who happened to cross his path. The wealth of scenarios he enacted for one or another of these women goes beyond imagination. His only desire was to satisfy them all. He had mastered the art of disguising his own reality to the point of changing his character when going from one to the other. That was the only way he had found to simultaneously fulfill the diversity of all their tastes and dreams.

This facility at becoming a different person also implied that he had never been able to be himself. An only son of a mother who continued to exist exclusively for him, during his childhood he held the overwhelming role of being the sole support for his mother's entire imagination. He was the one and only center of all her dreams, and he seemed to continue in this direction as an adult, being able to do nothing but honor all the women of creation with his body and his dreams. From what he said, he didn't seem to have the slightest idea what it meant to be himself. On the contrary, he was a master of changing who he was in order to satisfy the other. As he didn't have any reason to complain about his virility, Don Juan couldn't explain why he felt so at odds with himself. He was timid when he came to consult me, dreading that therapy would bring into question a sexual freedom that was his only passion, yet his inability to settle down with any of the numerous women in his life was beginning to bother him.

I asked him about his father. He described him as a taciturn and melancholic man with whom he had never had the slightest formative relationship. His father had a military career, but retired after an unfortunate accident that occurred during maneuvers. He came out of the accident slightly paralyzed in one leg, and his early retirement threw him into a deep depression with religious overtones. Little by little, he retreated from the world, spending the better part of his time closed up in his room, brooding in the dark or reading theology. He not only turned away from his son, but also from his wife, and very early in life Don Juan became his mother's only emotional support.

She herself had been wounded by life. Prior to seeing her husband fall into a total indifference to things of this world, she had seen her three brothers die during the war. She was thus the last surviving sibling. In addition, she had been preceded by two baby girls, both of whom had died shortly after birth. Her three brothers left behind a very numerous and entirely female progeny. Don Juan was the only male descendent of the maternal lineage. Beginning in his early teenage years, he structured his strangely generous phallicity with this triple collection of cousins.

He had already been seeing me for quite some time when a dream—quite an ordinary one coming from a man—inordinately disturbed him. In his dream, he saw himself making love to his mother. No other image accompanied this frightening vision; no association allowed him to tell me more. He could see in this dream only an alarming revelation of the insanity of his desire. He seemed in deep despair and cursed himself. For the first time since he started consulting me, Don Juan played the scenario of a man overwhelmed by shame.

Somewhat taken aback at seeing this valorous defender of eroticism being so torn apart by the revelation of an oedipal desire, I clumsily tried to tell him that this kind of dream was the privilege of all men. He broke down in tears. "No, you don't understand anything, this dream isn't an old desire. Now I know, it's a perfectly current desire. I can feel it. My entire sex life is nothing but an attempt to hide it." He was again on the verge of tears. "Now I know," he added before falling to pieces like a child.

My attempt to talk to him had placed me in the position of an impotent father. That was the only sense he could make of my words. "I understand," he moaned, "you've never been confront-ed with such an unbelievable case." He positioned me as a father who was incapable of forbidding the obscenity of his desire—a position that he confirmed in the following weeks. Although pre-viously his dreams had been as rich as the scenarios that accom-panied his love-making, after the fateful session Don Juan dreamt of only one thing: making love to his mother. Night after night, this same dream came back with a frightening monotony that paralyzed his normally impressive imagination. Only wanting to see the truth of his own desire, the lucid daytime consciousness of this monstrous nocturnal activity left him deeply downcast. He lost all taste for erotic games. In my presence, he bemoaned my incapacity to help him in this strange destiny to which he saw his desire drive him.

He was acting like a phobic child, crying "wolf" and pointing at his mother's sex as if it were the lair of a dreaded, fearsome desire. He now seemed to use my couch only as a place to collapse where, by casting me in the image of his father, he came to confess an impossible pain. He accused himself of never having felt any real desire outside the incestuous one he had tried to mask for so long. This didn't keep him from clinging to me like a life buoy. I was the one who revealed to him the source of his suffering, but he seemed to also want me to remain incapable of anything other than help-lessly and silently contemplating his terrible destiny.

In previous sessions, his dreams had brought to mind several scenes from his childhood. One, in which his mother was organizing children's games with his numerous cousins, reminded him of his early discovery of sexuality and the tricks that he later, as a teenager, rapidly imagined in order to go from one to the other cousin in the same night. At the time, I had suggested that this harem of cousins had, at a very early age, relieved him of his mother's massive and somewhat overbearing grip over him. The dream of making love to his mother had thus sprung up as a response to my words. From then on, Don Juan seemed to channel all his energy into proving to me that this dream was, as he had read in Freud, the product of an unconscious desire. The way in which the dream relentlessly repeated itself appeared to be more the reminiscence of a traumatic event. But what event?

Don Juan seemed to have me embody nothing but a helpless commander. I tried to find a lever by remarking that he had never really spoken to me about his father's sexuality. He began by protesting, arguing that I was turning him away from his own associations and concluding that, in any case, he had told me everything there was to know about his father. "No," I said, "you don't seem to have any representations of who your father was before his accident." The subsequent silence implied that my words had an effect.

He was a little older than 4 at the time of his father's accident. Not only were there no lingering memories of this period, but he also had no idea at all about his father's sexuality before his parents met. Don Juan remembered that one day he had angered one of his cousins, Natasha, who screamed at him that he was exactly like his father: nothing more than a horrible womanizer. Another time, this same Natasha told him that her mother had been his father's mistress. He hadn't paid any attention to this temperamental woman's gossip, but now that he thought about it, he wondered if Natasha hadn't been telling the truth. The idea seemed to amuse him. "In any case, if Dad had been Aunt Bronchka's lover, he wasn't the only one."

I reminded him that I had never heard anything at all about this aunt. He described her as a cultivated, worldly woman who loved life. She was the exact opposite of his own mother, and that explains her poor reputation in the family. She was criticized because too many men followed her husband's death. Although he had not seen her for a long time, he had always had an excellent relationship with her, and while it seemed impossible for him to question his mother about his father's sexuality he seemed at ease asking his aunt to verify the information that Natasha, her daughter, had told him. That's what Don Juan did. He visited his aunt and at the following appointment was even more distressed. He had unwittingly discovered the horrible key that unlocked the mystery of his fantasies.

His aunt was still lively. The aging and talkative woman was thrilled to answer his questions. She understood perfectly well that he wanted to hear about his father's youth and she quickly drew a portrait that was strangely different from the man he had known. She described him with a great many images of an adventurous, young, and gallant officer who was greatly appreciated by women. Don Juan received this unfamiliar vision of his father with an odd sensation of pain in his belly. Drowning in the verbal flow he had loosed, he felt worse and worse. In order to gather his wits, he focused on the object of his visit and tried, clumsily, to get her to admit an adventure with his father. She didn't seem to understand. Obsessed by the idea that this adventure could have taken place during his own childhood, he asked her what happened to his father at that time. The verbal flow was interrupted: "You mean," she sighed, "that terrible accident that left him impotent?"

When he heard that, Don Juan felt like he had been struck by lightning. What was even stranger was that, at the same time, he had the impression he had known it all along. His aunt had mentioned it without even doubting that he knew. How could she imagine that his own father's tragedy had been hidden from him? In talking to me, he glimpsed another perspective as to why talking about sex had been taboo throughout his childhood. He opened his child's eyes to the tragedy that his father had experienced and at the same time, he stopped bemoaning his fate.

This visit to his old aunt not only put an end to his lamentations over my inability to help him, it also put an end to his obsession over a desire to make love to his mother that he had taken for truth. The repetitive dream never renewed itself. Don Juan was able to understand how the distinctive features of his fantasies had crystallized. He had been 4½ years old at the time of the accident and although his parents had hidden the tragedy from him, the child had understood it quite well on an unconscious level.

On his mother's side of the family—and with the women of her family—he clearly saw what had happened. As his mother had already invested him with the role of the last male descendent of her lineage, he suddenly became the last sexually valid man of that lineage. Mourning their husbands, and having nothing but daughters, his mother's two other sisters-in-law had contributed to this massive, unconscious investment in his crotch. One could almost say that these two aunts, who had a bad opinion of the frivolities of the third, had literally pushed their daughters to adore this only male child. From there, he had only to take a small step—to respond to his cousins' advances—in order to assume this role of the still-potent descendent, ready to prove it through his sexual prowess.

On his father's side, Don Juan took longer to understand how the mechanisms of this fantasy structure had crystallized. First of all, he had to rediscover the idealized image that he had of his father during the first years of his life, an image that the accident had relegated to the bottom of his unconscious mind. That is the reason he felt ill at ease when his aunt spoke to him about his young and handsome father, whom he thought he had never known. The portrait she drew recalled images he had forgotten. A new series of dreams highlighted the passion for his father he had when he was very young and what a tragedy it had been for him to see his father suddenly retire from the world. Then he understood the source of the compulsive and repetitive dimension of his sexuality. That spot where sexuality acted on him, rather than him acting on his sexuality, seemed like an unconscious attempt to have that great seducer—his father—live on through him. This realization was stranger to him than everything else he discovered hidden behind his seemingly great sexual freedom.

In his father's lineage, the men's sexuality seemed to have been maneuvered by the ghosts of fathers past. When Don Juan's father was injured, he was the same age at which his own father had died. This grandfather disappeared at the prime of his life in a train accident. We see here the origin of a repetition. That is how Don Juan explained why his father had hidden his tragedy. Surviving his accident, his father had considered himself more dead than alive. He had certainly considered suicide, but had not wanted to impose on his son the terrible pain he himself had experienced from the disappearance of his own father. Finding nothing but religion as a support to brood over his misfortune, he had succeeded only in focusing his son's unconscious on the terrible destiny of the men of his family and, come puberty, Don Juan found himself carrying the duty of remedying this injustice.

As soon as he discovered his father's ghost in the compulsive and unsatisfactory dimension of his sexuality, Don Juan began to feel better about himself. Having re-inscribed his sexuality in his paternal lineage, he was able to discover in himself the first sparks of a desire to have children of his own.

3 The Making of the Male Sex

Nineteenth century sexuality, or the epitome of sexual barbarism

It is difficult to evaluate the impact of Freud's discoveries without at least briefly situating him in the context of the history of sexuality in the Western world. Contrary to popular belief, sexuality was far less problematic in the Middle Ages than in the nineteenth century. Western culture has inherited a puritanism resulting primarily from the rise of the bourgeois middle class, whereas the nobility had experienced a far less hampered sexuality, as demonstrated by the following period document.

Heroard was young Louis XIII's private doctor at the Bourbon court. Every day, he took scrupulous note of the events that occurred in the dauphin's life, which is how we know that, from a very young age, the dauphin accompanied the entire court to watch his royal parents'—Henry IV and Marie de Médicis—lovemaking. On January 1, 1603, when Louis XIII was just over 3 years old, Heroard wrote the following: "Carried into the Queen's chambers where the King joined them and the dauphin saw the King lay with her several times" (Heroard 1971). The sexual freedom that existed at the French court went hand in hand with a greater freedom of expression. Heroard describes the young dauphin as a child who frequently played with his "sparrow" and who spoke easily about it to his entourage. Our culture's sexual puritanism only arose later, becoming firmly established during the nineteenth century.

Just prior to the French Revolution, the bourgeoisie began to produce its own intellectual leaders who advocated an absurd and unreasonable sexual repression. The beginning of the eighteenth century brought the publication of the first book on the dangers of masturbation that slowly unleashed on Europe a gale of anti-masturbatory madness whose effects we can still feel today. *Onania, or the Heinous Sin of Self-Pollution, And all its Frightful Consequences, in both sexes, Considered* (Gay 1984), by an English clergyman was followed in 1758 by a book written by the Swiss physician Dr. Tissot, entitled *Onanism, dissertation on illnesses produced by masturbation*. Reprinted until 1905, this book opened the way for a whole genre of literature expounding on the dangers of sex. Doctors and teachers united to quell teenage sexuality. Numerous nineteenth-century secondary schools granted more time to the struggle against masturbation than to education itself. Draconian measures were advocated to cure "self-pollution" and "excessive lustfulness," including infibulation, castration, and clitorectomy. In Europe in 1882, Dr. Zambaco recommended cauterizing the clitoris with a hot iron. In 1894, Dr. Pouillet preferred to burn the entire surface of the vulva with silver nitrate so that, after the intervention, the slightest rub caused intense pain. The same year in Ohio, Dr. Eyer proceeded with a clitorectomy when a 7-year-old girl had persisted in her ways, tearing the sutures that had tied down her clitoris.

It was not until 1912 and the creation of the first psychoana-
lytical society that masturbation began to be once again considered normal during childhood and adolescence. Prior to that,
Victorian ideologists only recognized children's sexuality in order
to better repress it. At the time, Western culture remained
unaware of the way in which children develop their mental structures through investigating their sexuality.

A mask of morality and decorum allowed nineteenth century
teachers to initiate children into a perverse sexuality in all good
conscience. Before children were even aware of what it was,
teachers repressed masturbation by taking control over the children's bodies, giving free rein to their own sadistic urges. When
children are thus assaulted, they understand perfectly well the
sexual nature of the cruelty imposed on them. They can try to
cancel out this violence by according it a sexually pleasurable
meaning, like the children who laugh when their fathers whip
them. But in their fantasies, they conclude that adult sexuality is
fundamentally sadistic.

The impact of the mother tongue on a child's sexual development

Freud's greatest contribution was to define childhood as a formative period for sexuality. Humans are born premature. Like other
species, they are physically premature—the brain cells are not
fully formed until the age of 3, to which is added a psychic prematurity upon which depends the development of what we call
the mind. The latter constructs itself in relationship to a mother
tongue: a system of representations that associates words with
feelings and images. Before being born, the fetus is no more aware
of this system of representations than of the existence of air.
Although able to easily differentiate between sounds that are
inside or outside the womb, these sounds are only musical. The
fetus can hear words, but cannot associate them with any images.

We acquire our image- and word-based representations after birth. In order to resolve the problem of psychic prematurity, human beings use a mother tongue like a placenta: to nourish the formation of the psyche and, thus, of sexual fantasies.

It is difficult to conceive of the human psyche independently of the language and system of representations that shape it. The imagination and the particularities developed by the psyche that differ from one person to another depend on how each individual establishes himself or herself in this placenta of words provided by the first formative language. Erotic fantasies are no exception to this rule. This is exactly what the Freudian Oedipus theory brings to light: it explains the way in which childhood is a sexually formative period during which the little man imagines sexual relations with his parents and thus develops the system of fantasies that will be his own come adulthood.

The majority of adults, however, have no memories of their childhood sexual investigations. In addition, the few memories that do linger do not necessarily appear to them to be questions of sexuality, which explains why Freud's discovery of infantile sexuality provoked scorn from many of his contemporaries.

According to Freudian theory, there is nothing astonishing about the majority of adults forgetting their infantile sexuality. Freud puts forth that this forgetting—called repression—belongs to the process of human development and plays a dynamic role. Repression keeps people from remaining eternally in childhood, which is why a person will relegate to the bottom of his unconscious the fact that, in his childhood fantasies, his parents had been, generally speaking, his first sexual partners.

There exists another explanation for the rarity of early childhood memories. Childhood memories are selective and generally recount only the particular aspects of a child's links to this psychic placenta, the mother tongue. As a general rule, people do not remember anything that happened prior to their beginning to talk. A child registers his or her first memories when able to appropriate the use of words. In addition, these memories are, for the most part, reconstructed memories that summarize the way in which we fit ourselves into a system of representations. Freud called this kind of memory a screen memory. He identified screen memories by the fact that we visualize ourselves with the traits of the children we were, which indicates that they are not real memories but memories reconstructed at a later time using the same processes that are used in fantasy formation.

Deprived of the possibility of playing with his mother, a child reinterprets the event by incorporating the power of the "I" responsible for desire: in his fantasies, he is the one who deprives her of this pleasure. In the same manner, memories settle around an image in which we see ourselves. Sexual fantasies place the person who produces them at the center of the representations that evoke the other's pleasure. Reconstructed memories preserve the way we fit ourselves into a system of representation belonging to others, by adding to it an image of ourselves.

Therefore, the formation of fantasies by which the child gives himself an image of his own sex depends on his mother tongue and on the vocabulary used by his parents. These parents' inability to verbalize the reality of their sexuality becomes the first disturbance in the child's sexual development. "We don't talk about that," a mother says to her 3-year-old son when he approaches the public bench where she sits and asks, "Why is my wee-wee hard?" "It shouldn't be!" she repeats nervously, as if trying to keep herself from being at a loss. The child doesn't move. He's astonished. His obvious shock derives from his discovery that his mother does not possess words to verbalize a bodily action.

This absence of words creates gaps in a child's system of sexual representations. The gaps a child faces in his mother tongue generate sexual inhibitions and perversions in adulthood. When parents cannot, or will not, talk about the way they themselves deal with sexuality and death, they sentence their children to having no other recourse than their own imaginations in order to formulate an idea of the role sex plays in human relations.

For example, if a mother, incapable of words, turns and slaps her son at the first question he asks about his erections, the boy has but a very short step to take toward a perverse organization in his male urges. Rational thought and fantasy oppose each other: rational thought enables the faculty of judgment, fantasy enables sexual functioning. It allows us to imagine ourselves as possible actors in another person's pleasure. When the boy is slapped, he has difficulty integrating this event using exclusively rational thought. He could, of course, think that his mother was overwhelmed or tired, but if he thinks this, he no longer plays any role in the slap he received. If this slap is linked to a bodily action, a bodily pleasure, or, better yet, an erection, it automatically triggers the formation of fantasies. This is his only means of considering himself active in the slap that he received.

In fantasies, all punishment can turn into the proof of his parent's love for him and an assurance of the bodily pleasure bonding them to him. Having received a slap because his member was hard, the boy will conclude—in his fantasies—that the hardness of the penis is due to the meanness that characterizes men. At the same time, he will understand that his mother is wary of men's meanness—or hardness—to the same extent that she desires it. In his fantasies, the slap will signal a pleasure of which he deprives his mother. But when he becomes a man, he runs the risk of not knowing what to do with his male urges because he will consider them sadistic urges.

If parents cannot, or will not, allow their child to imagine the parents' own relationship to adult pleasure, they constrain the child to developing erroneous sexual theories. Discovering that his mother does not have a penis, a child could understand it purely and simply as an absence. If words do not intervene to explain that men and women have different orifices at that spot, he could remain ignorant of the fact that his mother possesses an orifice complementary to the penis. If he hears that the penis plays a role in reproduction, he may first of all find that incomprehensible. Is Dad's urine that different from his own? A fixation on this question opens the door to urolagnia, the sexual fetish for urine. If he understands that his father uses his penis to penetrate his mother, but he doesn't know that his mother has her own sexual orifice, he will try to understand from the perspective of his own body and the orifices he is familiar with. Does Dad fertilize Mom through the mouth or the anus? Then he will invent a sexual model that only makes reference to the infantile pleasure that he experienced with his mother. But as an adult, he may tend to seek a mouth or an anus, rather than a vagina, for the use of his penis.

From there, the forms of perversion are as rich as the paintings of Hieronymus Bosch. This comparison is to be taken seriously. All bizarre aspects of human sexuality stem from the child's rich imagination when the mother tongue was unable to provide him with representations allowing him to concretely understand the reality of human sexuality.

Accepting the sexual organs and the relationship to the father

As soon as he can stand on his own two feet, a child enters into what is called the oedipal stage. This period, in which he integrates functional models for his adult sexuality, ends around the age of 7 or 8. Many cultures consider this age the end of an individual's first cycle of development. We call it the age of reason. Another period follows, during which sexual questions generally remain in the background. Group experiences take precedence, coupling with school to prepare the way for socialization. Freud called this lull in an individual's sexual development the latency period. Adolescence follows, and sex reappears with the freshness it had during the oedipal stage.

Don Juan's case revealed the complexity of the oedipal process through which the little boy constructs his sexuality. Yet by wanting to apply the Oedipus theory to the letter, this man only managed to inhibit his work with me. What we call the Oedipus complex is generally poorly understood. In Greek mythology, Oedipus was a hero whose destiny led him to kill his father and marry his mother. Freud perceived in this myth a model for sexual maturation that allows the boy to integrate the existence of sexuality by identifying with his father and fantasizing the ability to take over his father's place with his mother. It would be naive to believe that the boy could really want to eliminate his father. If that were the case, he would lose the object of identification represented by his father, which is precisely what allows him to fantasize himself in the position of an adult male before his mother. He would then only be able to fantasize himself as a child, and his oedipal maturation would be hindered.

In his therapy, Don Juan relived and rediscovered the love that allowed him to identify with a father by transferring onto me the childhood idealization of his father. At the beginning of our work together, he actually believed that he had never had any formative relationship with his father. He was still at this point when the repetitive dream of making love to his mother appeared. The emotional intensity he felt for his father before he was 4 years old was, until this point, nothing more than a forgotten and repressed early childhood experience, only visible in the way that he transferred it onto his therapist. He reacted in two ways: he either clung to me like a little child, terrorized by the impossible task implied by his incestuous desires, or he bemoaned the powerlessness that he attributed to me, slipping into a gloomy depression in which he relived an unconscious identification with his father.

How had his father's accident been traumatic for him? Certainly not with regard to his own virility. For the child, the trauma lay in the lack of words and the mystery of their relationship to sex. The accident led to an absence of all talk about sex, suddenly taboo, and this kept Don Juan from continuing to idealize his father as a sexual being. Only one third party existed to step between him and the ardent desire that his mother devoted to him by living for no one else: the battalion of cousins. Yet, in addition, he said himself that he had "learned to make love without ever having the slightest idea about its purpose." That is the meaning behind the insistent repetition of his dream. Although he wanted to understand his dream as the proof of his current adult desire, he acted like a whining child who had lost me as a father.

Freud considered the Oedipus complex inseparable from the castration complex, a term Freud used to designate the psychic maturation process that allows a person to acknowledge his or her biological sex—to accept being a man or a woman. However, one should not conclude that male imagination centers on the shame of losing this precious object represented by the penis, which is unfortunately the only meaning often given to this concept. Although a boy can experience difficulty accepting his sexual organ, it is not out of fear of losing it. When such fear arises, it is generated primarily by the difficulty that men have in conceiving of their penises as actually being one with their bodies. Erection and detumescence do not appear as voluntary actions, and boys tend to view their sexual organs as little people endowed with their own autonomy. An adult, and even more so a child, could find it difficult to apprehend all the implications of calling his penis *little soldier*, or even calling it *cock*.

In the relationship that sexually inhibited men have with their therapists, they continue to experience themselves as children, which enables them to dream that their penises detach from their bodies and travel through the air autonomously. These dreams do not mean that the man suffers from the fear that his cock will fly away. On the contrary, in these dreams, the sleeper's desire protests against the neurosis that inhibits his sexuality. The dream expresses the message that the penis is disconnected from the rest of the body. Men who have these dreams consider themselves awkward, inhibited, or unhealthily timid. They are not at all concerned about their virility, but feel incapable of approaching women, and therein lies their neurosis. In these cases, the dream does not express a fear of losing the penis, but a desire to see it take off—in short, *to get off* with somebody.

Male imagination easily represents the penis as separate from the body since men experience their organ as a vehicle that they must learn to master. Unless he had a father like the actor, Steve, in the previous chapter, whose craziness forbade any identification with an adult man, if an adult man jokingly menaces to cut off his penis a boy will tend to break out in laughter, because in his erotic imagination it evokes detumescence. A little girl witnessing this scene would find nothing funny in it. The boy laughs because he feels a man-to-man complicity concerning the way his penis functions. For him, it is one of the penis's special attributes to be, most of the time, *cut off* or separated from the astonishing ability to have an erection. In addition, as long as he has not reached sexual maturity, a boy cannot measure the real power of his sexual organ, and only through adult men can he imagine his own sexual future. He becomes preoccupied with the size of his penis because he feels *cut off* from it, or lacking a penis, of which he cannot really take possession until adolescence. Moreover, he stops verifying its length as soon as he makes love and discovers the actual scope of the sexual act.

The little man can only accept his penis if able to imagine this organ's role in adulthood. Yet to reach this stage, he must first renounce the advantages of the other sex. Pride in being a boy first of all requires admitting the impossibility of possessing a belly as powerful as his mother's. Men's castration anxieties therefore very frequently center on their bellies, as we saw with Don Juan. When his aunt drew him a portrait of a father he had completely forgotten, he was not overcome with shame, or an hysterical pain in his testicles, but with a pain in his belly, there to remind him that he was built in the image of his father.

If accepting one's own sexual organ were self-evident, transexuality—the desire some men have to be surgically transformed into women—would not exist. Recognition and acceptance of his biological sex is dependent upon the ways the child's psyche links to the placenta that is, for him, the mother tongue. Based on what his parents tell him about his biological sex and the representations they provide, a child structures the framework of his desire, and accepts—or does not accept—the implications of being male or female.

Sexuality cannot be constructed solely in a drive-oriented relationship with an adult of the opposite sex. Its construction requires an idealizing identification with an adult of the same sex. A child's sexual health therefore expresses itself through a proud idealization of the characteristics with which his parents consider his sexual future. From this perspective, gender-preoccupied behaviors or beliefs, such as machismo or radical feminism, could be viewed as nothing more than an adult resurgence of what hindered the child's matter-of-course idealization of his or her own sex.

The father's sexual organ: a lever of sexual maturity

Freud placed a boy's incestuous desires at the center of his questions about sexuality, but more importantly, he also indicated that *idealization of the father's sexual organ is the actual lever required for a boy's sexual maturation*. Moreover, a male child can only produce or verbalize fantasies in which he takes his father's place beside his mother on the condition that his father not only be alive, but also be solidly established in his mother's bed. If the boy cannot idealize his father, because his father is ill or neurotic or because his parents no longer relate sexually, he cannot produce these fantasies, because they would be too threatening.

Being limited to fantasizing oneself in a dual relationship with the mother results in the primary handicap to sexual maturation for both sexes. Normally, we characterize children's sexuality as polymorphous, meaning that pleasure takes on several forms, be it through the mouth or the anus or any other part of the body that gives pleasure. A human being discovers sexuality in the carnal relationship with his or her mother. After having felt the reality of pleasure with her, a boy must take a second step towards realizing that he cannot sexually satisfy her. This realization occurs in his relationship to men and in the discovery of their role in reproduction. When he learns that his very existence originates from his father's penis, a little boy finds a model for his future. He then idealizes his penis's adult function and turns his back on the infantile sexuality that he experienced with his mother. This is the process of oedipal maturation.

Any time spent with little boys reveals that their all-time favorite games are playing guns, rockets, and spaceships. As soon as a boy realizes sexuality's adult role, continuing infantile modes of pleasure contradicts his ideals, now focused on adulthood. Kissing or playing with little girls doesn't interest him any more. He could, of course, play doctor with them, but as soon as he becomes aware of his sexual prematurity, and at the same time of his adult future, a boy turns away from these kinds of games, calling them "baby games." He means that, in view of his future condition as a man, he finds no interest in continuing to play doctor for an infantile pleasure that he has already experienced with his mother. Playing with guns and missiles is another story because he can now fantasize himself in possession of a fabulous object with the power of life and death, thus projecting into the future an image of his sexual organ capable of engendering life. At this age, little boys prefer to play among themselves.

In a consultation, a 4-year-old boy told me the story of a king and a queen who could not get along together: "You see, the king was king, so he had everything. He had a conversion machine to go to the stars. The queen didn't have anything. That's why she's not happy." Responding to my astonished look, he said, "No, she had a mouth, she had nothing. She's a queen who loves cakes. So the king had an idea. He asked his conversion machine—it's a conversion robot that talks. With his conversion machine the king went to all the stars at the same time, and the machine knew all the stars that had cake stores. That was the idea. After that, the queen was happy. She liked it when the king drove her with his machine. She had all the star cakes and she ate lots."

Another 6-year-old boy played on the floor in my office and pretended not to pay any attention to me while he playfully and assuredly hit the floor with one hand and announced: "It's men who make noise. They make firecrackers, thunder, and lightning." He stopped, as if astonished by what he had just said and added, as if asking himself a question, "But ladies—what do they do?"

This is how little boys express the very high ideal they have of adult sexual organs. Incredible arms, lightning, and thunder recount how they idealize the power of this sex. The conversion machine is another version, and no better one exists for the male organ in operation. The commercial success of toys becomes clear in this perspective.

Thus, at a very young age, a boy turns his back on the pleasures he experienced with his mother. Oral and anal sexuality appear derisory and of little interest compared to an adult man's sexuality, which, in the image of God, can perpetuate life. Of course, for this to happen, he has to have been informed of the penis's role in reproduction. There is nothing seriously wrong in forbidding a child's questions by answering with stories of snails, puppy-dog tails, and storks, but it doesn't help him to resolve his own queries.

Between the ages of 1 and 7, questions about sex are a daily part of a child's maturation. Where do babies come from? What's that noise my parents make at night? Why does Mommy prefer to sleep with Daddy instead of me? Why does she lock the door when she is alone with him? All are questions that he answers himself with real or imaginary responses, or with fantasies. He concentrates his responses in games and dreams from which he will build the fantasies that will serve as a background to his adult sexuality. The boy can easily imagine himself in the skin of a hero with his father's sexual strength saving widows and orphans in distress. Riding a motorcycle, he has a strength between his legs that takes him in the right direction. As a fireman, he will put out the flames of desire. As a soldier, he assassinates the demons of his infantile sexuality.

A boy's need to idealize his father's sexual organ during the oedipal stage stems from the fact that he cannot measure his own real strength simply by referring to his own body. An erection can, of course, produce pleasure at a very young age, but if the boy cannot make sense of the pleasure that his organ produces it may be experienced as burdensome. "Why is my wee-wee hard?" the little boy asks his mother. If he discovers that she cannot provide words in response, then guilt may accompany masturbation, signalling a complete absence of meaning in the pleasure the child has discovered. Yet the child does not need to be told about the pleasureful aspects of sex: having discovered bodily pleasure in his relationship to his mother, he has no need to be informed of the reality of pleasure. On the other hand, based exclusively on the way his child's body functions, he cannot understand the male role in reproduction. This is the information he needs. If the role his father's penis played in giving him life is hidden from him, he will remain unable to develop awareness of his own genital immaturity, and will be unable to differentiate adult sexuality from what he already knows, which is anal and oral. His sexual development runs the risk of being hindered. The only recourse he will have in order to provide himself with a model for adult sexuality is to project the oral and anal basis of his own sexuality onto his parents. Isn't that what can be seen in perversion—a confusion in the functions of all the bodily orifices?

Clearly, the possibility of idealizing his father's sexual organ serves as the most important lever to a boy's sexual maturation. If he can recognize that this sex is responsible for his own existence, a boy can then imagine his own sex capable of performances other than those he already knows. Being able to project himself, through his father, into an idealization of adult sexuality allows him, at the same time, to turn away from the infantile pleasure that he experienced with his mother, permitting a transition into the latency stage, during which he will be able to withstand the wait for the adult sexuality upon which he has projected his ideals.

Case study: a rubber fetish, or the impossibility of idealizing the father's sexual organ

Built like a Schwarzenegger, about 35 years old and fairly handsome, Peter seemed very uncomfortable about having made an appointment with me. He had never spoken to anybody about his fetish. He had always gotten by with it, but his wife couldn't cope any longer. Had she not insisted, he would not have felt the need to consult me, but for the past few months she could no longer bear wearing the rubber aprons he needed in order to desire her sexually.

At the beginning she accepted this particularity of his sexuality, but over time she ended up becoming jealous of the plastic and rubber aprons he liked so much. He had a large collection that he had gathered during his travels. The mystery of his sexuality resided in the need for this texture—"first of all cool and exciting, and rapidly very hot and humid to the touch"—which was indispensable for him to experience real sexual pleasure. He could make love without this contact, but he would only feel bland pleasure and could only ejaculate by mentally imagining its presence.

As if he were burdened by his big build, Peter blushed when he spoke to me about his sexuality, leaving the impression of being a

child who had grown up too fast. He had, in fact, discovered masturbation at an early age. From his very early childhood, and
without any interruption, he used a vast panoply of plastic and
rubber objects to satisfy a masturbatory urge that, although compulsive, had never caused him any problems. He nevertheless did
reach a marriageable age without having the slightest idea about
sexuality's role in producing children. He was greatly disturbed
when a friend his own age finally told him. During the same period, he met the woman who would become his wife. She was as
ignorant as he was about the end product of sexual games. For
more than a year, they had a platonic relationship before Peter
dared to propose reciprocal masturbation. He then initiated her
into his erotic tastes, they married, had two children, and were
very happy. Aside from his wife, I was the first person he had
talked to about his sexuality.

When I first listened to him, I thought that masturbation
played a central role in his sexual organization, so I asked him.
"Perhaps," he responded with a childish laugh. "As far back as I
can remember, I see myself masturbating. My first memory is of
me lying on my little bed with diapers and rubber pants. My
mother just changed me and I was waiting for her to leave in
order to lie back and masturbate by wriggling on my belly." He
was smiling now, remembering a very happy childhood. I tried to
learn more about his parents.

His mother came from a rather poor mining family and had
waited until she was 18 before turning her back on the fate of the
women in her family. She wanted to escape the stagnant resigna-
tion with which she saw her mother and grandmother both shoul-
der the premature loss of their men from silicosis. Running away
from this sad destiny, she moved to the city, where she found a
cleaning job in a hospital that allowed her to go to school to
become a nurse. Then she met Peter's father. He had an honest
job, and he didn't want his wife to work. She happily abandoned

her work at the hospital in order to step up the social scale through this marriage.

From then on, she seemed to have only one desire: to be the perfect middle-class wife. She invested as much energy into keeping her home and herself as she did in her son. Peter spoke of his mother as appearance-conscious and playful in her way of dressing, just as she was meticulous, organized, and fussy about keeping up her household. In fact, it seems that she had compensated for the guilt of abandoning her own mother by investing an obsessional energy into the household tasks, of which her son's education was the major element. Until the age of 9, when the stork dropped a little sister, Peter had been excessively doted on by his mother. He described with humor the shining wood floors that he could walk on only with slippers and the pranks he used to play on his mother by disturbing her so-cherished orderliness.

On the other hand, Peter didn't seem to have anything to say about his father. People always told him that he looked like his father, and that is where he got his impressive build. But he never found any affinity with his father. They lived together, not really like strangers, but without either of them ever really feeling the need to talk to each other. He had the impression he loved his father, but he really couldn't find anything else to add to that. After a moment of silence, he returned to his mother.

"Since you want to know about my parents, I have to tell you that my mother had a large wardrobe of beautiful clothes. She also had a nice collection of rubber aprons like those she used at the hospital and some other plastic ones with pretty designs. She loved anything that was modern. She used to proclaim their hygienic qualities, and I must have been sensitive to that very early. In any case, she never did anything in the house without first putting on one of those beautiful aprons. To take care of me and wash me, she generally put on a large apron made of soft white rubber. Very early, I perceived the delicate touch of rubber. She used to get furious when I wet my bed, and after washing me and changing the sheets she laid me over her knees to give me a little spank. I already loved the cold, damp contact of the rubber against my penis, and I very quickly noticed that the spank created a delicious rubbing sensation. After each bath, my mother also took me on her knees, the other way around, in order to correctly clean my penis. She pulled back the foreskin to clean the glans and also to avoid my having to be circumcised. Of course, when she did that, I always got an erection. . . ."

As he seemed to allude to it, I noted that his mother practically masturbated him. "Yes," he said, thoughtfully, "I knew she liked it, but whenever I starting moving my legs with pleasure, she forbade it. As she said it was bad, one day I asked her why. Then she told me some story about women and girls that I didn't understand.

"Later, after I met other children at nursery school, I asked her one day when she was cleaning me if you also pull back girls' skin. That is when I learned that women didn't have penises, just a hole. I was shocked. I remember it well. I had the impression that I had just learned something really incredible."

I asked him about his father's position on the circumcision story. He didn't have the slightest idea. "No, another time, a little later, my father caught me masturbating. I must have been 7 or 8; my sister wasn't born yet. I understood that he wanted to talk to me, and I waited for him. He thought for a long time before pronouncing the only sermon that he ever gave me in my life. He explained to me that it was bad, that little boys shouldn't do this thing, that it could harm them. I concluded that it was reserved for girls. That did not make me want to stop. I masturbated even more, thinking about the girls and women who had the right to make themselves feel so good. I saw them reaching seventh heaven in fantastic rubber aprons. I was already pilfering my mother's aprons in order to masturbate. I didn't feel guilty. I told myself that if I continued like this, they would end up taking me to the hospital, and doctors and beautiful nurses wearing rubber aprons would make me masturbate until my penis disappeared definitively and I would become a girl."

This interview gave me enough information to be able to understand the origins of his fetish, and it illustrates fairly well what we have just discussed. In his earliest screen memory he sees himself wearing rubber pants. The fact that he sees himself indicates that it is a reconstructed memory. Associated with early masturbation, rubber summarizes the thoughts he, as a child, used to fit himself into the system of sexual representations used by the adults around him, particularly by his mother.

Rubber served as an erotic third party that allowed the child to fantasize himself as the main actor in the pleasure that his mother was supposed to have in taking care of him. Associated with cleaning up and with masturbation, strangely enough, it also acted as the major representation of maternal femininity. He considered rubber aprons to be part of his mother's nice wardrobe. He talked about his mother's consciousness about her appearance, thus summarizing the representation that the child gave to femininity. In his fantasies, the aprons became the seductive tool used by girls, women, or nurses who "reach seventh heaven in fantastic rubber aprons."

This strange role attributed to rubber originates in the fact that his mother's aprons were accessories to an early eroticism that he had not been able to metabolize and make sense of through words. His mother made a fetish of cleanliness by obsessionally masturbating her son, but refused to consider it an act of pleasure. Furthermore, her aprons had the power to transform spankings into delicious erotic sensations.

Here we see fantasies forming. The child knew that his mother used aprons for household tasks that, in and of themselves, have nothing erotic about them. But as far as he was concerned, he did not associate them with his mother's disgust for excrements, but integrated them into the pleasure that he was supposed to produce for his mother when she cleaned him. He could not conceive of the idea that she would not get intense pleasure out of cleaning his penis. Moreover, as an adult, he remained convinced of it. Logically thinking, a rubber apron protects from dirt. In fantasies, it protected his mother from the too-great pleasure that she had with her child.

We see how denial sets in. Denial is an important concept in psychotherapy. *Denial results from the way in which fantasy formation infiltrates logical thinking and shows up as faulty judgment.* While one truth is recognized by rational thought, another level of the unconscious cancels out this truth in order to avoid bringing into question the person's fantasy construction. On one hand, this man knew that his mother had raised him with a horrible, obsessional rigidity and that the sight of excrement was her foremost obstacle to any kind of pleasure. On the other hand, he seemed to continue to believe that his mother liked rubber because she was afraid of experiencing too much pleasure from his penis. The thought processes that engender denial are natural in children, but denial only establishes itself in a child's psychic and sexual development to the extent to which that child appropriates the denials found in his surrounding environment.

His mother knew she was masturbating her son. Moreover, this hygienic masturbation was designed to prepare him for adulthood by avoiding circumcision, so naturally the child asked questions about his sexuality. She tried to answer as best she could, but when she saw him feeling pleasure, she didn't register that his questions could possibly relate to the pleasure she gave him. In order to avoid feeling like an incestuous mother, she forbade him from moving his legs and expressing the pleasure he felt. The child concluded that it was normal to feel pleasure with his mother, but bad to express it. He asked why, but got only answers he could not understand. His mother did not take advantage of the situation to start him thinking about the way his sex functioned by, for example, sending him to ask his father about the supposed risks he ran being circumcised. She talked to him about women and girls instead. He therefore heard nothing but talk of her own incestuous guilt, and he could not understand a word of it.

There is no better example of maternal denial. She knew she was masturbating her son, but denied the pleasure she felt. It was a duty, like the other household tasks represented by the apron.

This apron represents the way in which maternal denial inhibited this child's psychic development. Taking the place of what the child perceived as sexual representations of his mother, it represents a fault in judgment, a mental barrier that his childhood sexual investigations could not cross. It inhibited the child's mental development by eliminating precisely what Freud called the castration complex.

Caught in a vicious circle of incest and guilt, the mother eliminated representations of her adult femininity—her relationship to a penis other than her son's. She therefore led him to understand that his little penis was more important to her than the one that gave him life. She deprived her child of one of the most important moments in a boy's mental and sexual development: the moment when he has to realize the sexual immaturity of his penis.

To observe his penis's immaturity, the child needs to compare himself to an adult man capable of sexually satisfying his mother and giving her children, thus allowing him to scale the idealization of this caretaking goddess down to proportion by turning his idealization toward the man upon whom she depends sexually. In his fantasies, the boy can then identify with an adult man who satisfies the mother in other ways than a child would. He idealizes a kind of pleasure other than the one he experiences with her. That allows him to enter the latency stage and calmly await his biological maturity.

This springboard allows the child to leave the dual relationship with his mother. It is also what was missing in Peter's childhood, whose father didn't offer the slightest sexual figure with whom to identify. It would be too simple to believe that mothers are solely responsible for their children's sexual development. Let's examine the moment when Peter's father caught him masturbating.

From the child's point of view, this situation provided an obvious way to question his father about the way the penis functions. Having discovered the marvelous sensations, Peter wanted to know what his father thought and could teach him. By taking note of how long his father spent thinking before he spoke, Peter indicated that he had been impatiently awaiting his father's words. Then his father explained to him that masturbation was bad for boys' health. Again, the child could not understand. How could he, when his mother masturbated him regularly for his own good? He concluded that masturbation was a purely feminine activity, concerning only women and girls, which explained why his father seemed to be unaware of the way it works.

At the same time, the simple fact of possessing a penis became problematic for Peter. How is it that adult men don't know anything about these delicious sensations that he would have loved to hear his father talk about, unless they deprive themselves in order to keep their penises? Seeing nothing attractive about being a man, the child chose to identify with a girl rather than with his father, which is why he imagined beautiful nurses giving him pleasure and, by making him lose his penis, transforming him into a girl.

This child was unable to idealize his father's sexual functioning and could not be proud of his sex. During adolescence, Peter rediscovered sexuality as he understood it during the oedipal stage. When he met the woman he was to marry, he found nothing else to propose to her than reciprocal masturbation, which was nothing more than the incestuous autoeroticism of his childhood. Confronting his wife with this sexuality that he continued to imaginarily experience with his mother, he ended up making her jealous of a lousy rubber apron.

We have clearly seen how a father can be blind to the way in which his child absorbs maternal denial. If the father had simply explained the role the penis plays in reproduction, he could have entirely modified Peter's repertoire of sexual fantasies. If he is unable to idealize the adult function of the penis, a child has no reason to leave behind infantile pleasure. For an adult, sexual abstinence is understandable and admissible because the sexual organs are invested with the power of reproduction. Why would it be any different for a child?

4   Virility and the Importance of the Testicles

The testicles and naming the sexual organs

Under French royalty, the ladies of the court systematically filed past the cradle of the newly born dauphin, enraptured by the beauty and shape of his testicles. These women paid resounding tribute to the testes of this child destined for the throne because they symbolized the transmission of the royalty, and so custom had it that the sexual organs of the newly born prince be exposed to the view and comments of all.

Representation of the testicles plays a major role in the development of a boy's sexuality. As with the custom at the French court, their function in reproduction must be named. Not informing a child about the role played by the testicles in fertility equals depriving that child of the possibility of idealizing his father's sexual organs. It equals leaving that child—unable to imagine sexual maturity—to construct his sexuality at the risk of finding nothing to idealize but childish mechanisms for pleasure, as in Peter's case.

The little man is not ignorant of his erections, nor of the plea-sure they bring. As a baby, he can urinate with an erection, some-thing he can no longer do when he grows older. Yet, he cannot understand from the way his own body—a child's body—func-tions that his penis can produce anything other than urine. Whether or not his parents speak to him about his erections changes little with regard to the way he understands his penis. That is not the case with his testicles. *The testicles must be incor-porated into language in order for a child to be able to imagine his evo-lution into adult manhood.*

In a boy's unconscious body image, the testicles, far more than the penis, correspond to the vagina. A little girl's relationship to her clitoral sexuality resembles a boy's relationship to his penis. When a girl's mother cleans her between the legs, it gives her as much pleasure as it gives a little boy. Both identify that area as a specific erogenous zone. In order to be able to turn away from an infantile fixation on the mother, both the boy and the girl need to know that there exists a pleasure other than the infantile pleasure they experienced with her.

The discovery of her vagina is pivotal in a girl's sexual devel-opment. It represents a part of her body that her mother cannot enter and through which her mother cannot give her pleasure. In her unconscious body image, she views the vagina as a kind of chest or casket, a music box whose key her mother does not pos-sess. However, this occurs only if she has been made aware of the man's role in reproduction. What interests the little girl is know-ing that only men possess the key that can animate this music box and that entry is forbidden to her mother: this is the springboard that will allow her to project herself into the future.

So the idea that a man can penetrate her allows a girl to turn away from the infantile pleasures that she experienced with her mother. The representation a boy has of his testicles allows him this transition. As an adolescent, the fact of being full of semen obliges a boy to go looking for something other than what he has found with his mother. A girl needs to know that her vagina is forbidden to her mother; a boy must be able to imagine that the life-giving power harbored in his testicles—a power that will be available to him at adolescence—cannot be used by his mother. More than having a penis, or even having been able to experience its erogenous function with his mother, it is, as we say, "having balls" that signals to the boy his own destiny as a man with sexual organs.

Of course, how an adult individual makes use of his or her genitals is conditioned by unconscious knowledge. Thus, one cannot envision informing a child about sexuality through an educational model. Apprenticeship and education generate only conscious knowledge; they do not eliminate the fact that there exists an unconscious knowledge that governs what each person must reinvent. *Sex, by definition, is not learned, but reinvented with each generation.* Therefore, incorporating the sexual organs into language should not be confused with education, especially in the relationship with one's own children. The body must be incorporated into language. Bearing a name characterizes being human. The father's name inscribes a child into a succession of generations. Therefore, naming the testicles does not so much concern the child's testicles as it does those of the adult men with whom the child identifies himself. Let us look more closely at how naming the testicles relates to the conscious and unconscious representations with which a child's father experiences his own testicles.

Handing down the "family jewels"

Left unnamed, the testicles draw attention to themselves in other ways. Sometimes a child's testes refuse to lower into the scrotum, leading to a serious risk of sterility beyond adolescence. Yet this symptom can be healed by establishing an exchange of words between the father and the son. This is what we discovered with the therapeutic team of the Dijon Hospital for Psychotic Children where I worked for more than 10 years.

Generally speaking, psychotherapy can have surprising effects on the symptom of sterility. Several of my patients taught me that psychotherapy is one of the rare practices that can reverse a medical diagnosis of permanent sterility for women. In their therapy with me, these women, for whom celioscopy revealed tubal sterility, explored what had been handed down from mother to daughter concerning their genitality. None of them continued to use contraception, believing the diagnosis of irreversible sterility. Yet to everyone's surprise, they miraculously became pregnant, stumping their gynecologists, who could provide no explanation. So from these patients, and from the psychotic children with undescended testicles, I learned to what extent the mind governs reproduction down to its most somatic dimension.

When I was working at the hospital for psychotic children, an educator called me one day. Knowing that I had a child in therapy who had resolved the problem of his testes lowering, he wanted to ask me about this subject. He was responsible for five children, three of whom exhibited this same symptom: they were approaching puberty, and their testes had not yet lowered. The majority of other educators were women, and since he was one of the few men in the institution, he received most of the boys who, becoming pubescent, started creating problems for his female colleagues.

He had already spoken at length with the psychiatrist, who suggested he get my opinion because neither of them could find a satisfactory solution, nor could they resign themselves to being the passive witnesses to the beginnings of a sterility that would require the parents to consider surgery. A psychotic child always runs a greater risk of having a difficult experience with such an operation. In addition, we excluded the possibility of my intervening personally because these children were from families who had already vigorously opposed meeting with a psychoanalyst. So I proposed that we meet with the psychiatrist in order to discuss the problem among the three of us.

In listening to the two of them talk about these children, I was surprised to notice that the possibility of sterility seemed to concern only men, with the exception of the children's fathers: none of the three mothers nor any of the educators had ever mentioned the problem of sterility. As for the fathers, they stood out by their absence. They were practically never seen in the institution. As a result, the few men found in the institution felt called upon in the place of the fathers. That is exactly what was wrong, as this kind of problem is symptomatic of a lack of father–son transmission.

I mentioned that the decision to operate on a child could not be made by the institution. If such a decision were to be necessary, it was up to the fathers, and only the fathers, to assume the responsibility. Therefore, it was necessary to give them the means to express their opinions on this question. Considering the context, and in an effort to bring to light how this type of symptom concerned transmission from father to son, I proposed that the men make appointments with each father and son together, excluding the mothers as well as all the women who were part of the institution. It was not a good idea that I attend the meetings, but the psychiatrist and the educators did not need me in order to question the fathers about the way they had spoken to their children about sexuality. In that way, they would see if the children had heard anything about the role the testicles play in reproduction. It seemed to me that simply talking could have an effect. In any case, it would allow the fathers themselves to make a decision concerning their children's reproductive capacity.

A month later, after a meeting had been held with each of the fathers, we met to review the work. Out of the three children, two no longer had a problem. Their testes had lowered following the appointment. In each of the meetings, the psychiatrist and the two educators had been confronted with the same scenario: extremely moved by being questioned by men about the way they spoke to their children about sex, the fathers began by stuttering, as if they had not understood the question. One even turned bright red. All three finally came up with the same argument: "Well, he's seen animals." One of the educators responded that yes, certainly, but does he know what purpose the testicles serve, and, for that matter, do animals know? Such a simple question was enough to put things back into place. The discussion followed its course and a few days later, the children's testes had lowered.

What is interesting with such an example is that *we are not talking about intervening directly on the body, but about incorporating the body into language.* In these cases, what had a therapeutic effect upon the children were the questions that the fathers were asked concerning the place the testicles held in their thoughts about sex. Confronted by other men, the fathers stuttered and blushed because this question concerned them. In blushing and stuttering, they showed themselves to be like children who had been able to observe animals, but who were unable to clearly perceive the role of the testicles. Therefore, their own relationship to erection was disconnected from the testicles. When a father forgets his own testicles, he can no longer situate himself in a lineal relationship with his child.

The testicles witness a place in which virility creates the mother, which explains why they must be incorporated into language. Unrepresented testicles suggest that sexuality excludes reproduction and denies the fact that humans do *not* function like animals. So the relationship to the testicles must be transmitted from father to son. Called the *family jewels*, they represent a wealth bequeathed from man to man that can be used with women.

The story of the broken window and Daddy's balls

This is a story about a little 4-year-old boy who had trouble sleeping ever since his father came home drunk one night and broke a window. The child got anxious when it was time to go to bed, refusing to go to sleep, saying nothing but "My window is going to break." The father had himself gone through psychoanalysis and prior to consulting me had tried to calm the child. He explained to his son why he sometimes drank, but that had no effect. The child continued to be unable to fall asleep fearing that his window would break. It was not his father's window, nor the one that had been broken that kept the child from sleeping, but the fear that— or the desire to see—his own window be broken.

I saw the father, the mother, and the child together and then suggested that the father tell me more about the night he came home drunk and broke the window. "Nothing special happened that night," he said. "I came home from a dinner out feeling gloomy. My wife was sound asleep, and I must have already been completely drunk. I don't remember much. I think I poured myself another whiskey in the kitchen. That's when I broke the window and woke the little tyke up. I have no idea why I did it. I saw the moon through the window. It's like I was blaming the heavens or the moon, but I don't really understand why."

I approached the event as if it were a dream, asking him what he could associate with the kitchen, the window, the window pane, the sky, the moon, with all of the elements that lingered in his memory. He associated the kitchen with his mother, the window with birth, the sky with God the Father, and the moon with the way in which his mother referred to female genitals. However, he could not spontaneously associate anything with the window pane. The only thing that came to mind was an expression that his mother used frequently to have him behave himself, and this brought to mind all the accumulated grievances that he held against his mother. While he was talking about her, he suddenly seemed to understand what had happened the night he sent his fist through the window.

"In fact, I think that I was blaming the heavens or God. I was feeling really down. I felt terribly alone and, blaming the moon, I cursed the Creator. I held it against him for having made me a man. Even now I can see the moon scoffing at me from the other side of the window." I reminded him that he had associated the moon with female genitals. "Yes, you're right, that was an important question in my analysis. My mother spoke easily about girls' genitals, which she referred to as the "moon," but I never heard anything about boys' genitals. She was a strange person. I ended up thinking that she'd never liked men. I think that for her there only existed one sex, her own, and for a very long time I held her responsible for my father's death."

I gave them an appointment for the following week, but the father came alone, glowing because his son's insomnia had been resolved. In fact, he had only come to tell me what had happened. Two days after our appointment, he got drunk again and came home late. He must have made some noise, and the child woke up again. He tried to coax his son back to sleep, but the child kept asking all sorts of questions. As usual when he had been drinking, he only remembered half of what happened, but he remembered talking to his son for a long time, and vividly recalled giving his son a lesson in sexual anatomy. He pointed out on his belly the area where women have ovaries while explaining to him that men, like themselves, have testicles. In this way, he explained the complementarity of the sexual organs that allows children to be conceived. He remembered it all the more clearly because after that the child said he was tired and wanted to sleep. To the father's great surprise, the child went to sleep without any difficulty. The next day, while his father was still sleeping, the child ran up to his mother and said, "You know what? I've got balls. Daddy told me so!" Then and there his insomnia ceased.

This example illustrates how the symptoms from which children suffer are often nothing more than questions. Through his insomnia, this child was trying to query his father. The answers rid him of his difficulty sleeping. This is what happens when a child is assailed by questions he cannot even formulate, such as those provoked by this father's drunkenness.

What does a child see when the person he idealizes appears before him under the influence of alcohol, in a state that gives the impression he has lost control? The child sees a ghost, something beyond representation that seems to be driving the adult. Unable to put a name to this thing, he becomes filled with questions he cannot verbalize. Having seen his inebriated father, exhausted yet unable to sleep, the only way the child could formulate his question was through an unconscious identification with his father, which expressed itself through an inability to sleep.

Yet the ghost that persecuted the father was none other than the ghost of the father's own mother. That is what came to light in his work with me, at which the child was present. Both of his own parents were neurotic. In his own childhood, he had never been able to have a father who spoke to him as simply about sex as he had to his own son. Therefore, he hadn't had the slightest idea concerning the purpose of the testicles. From his mother, he heard that girls had "moons," but he had no equivalent. The sight of the moon through the window brought back to life an anger against his father's absence that had left him alone in an insoluble confrontation with his mother.

All traditions hold the moon as a symbol of feminine radiance, reflecting the sun's light, symbol of masculine radiance. The sun gives off light and life. His companion, the moon, reflects his strength once the night falls. The ovaries remain hidden inside the body, while the testicles must descend into the scrotum in order to reach maturity. Like the sun, they are visible. The ovaries are like the moon, lingering in the night of the body, appearing in their reproductive role only when lit up by the testicles' visibility. This anatomical difference, obliging the testicles to leave the inside of the body, is analogous to the differences between male and female drives. A man's sexual drive is turned outside his body, its purpose to expel semen. A woman's sexual drive is turned inside her body, towards receiving the male sexual organ. Such are the complementary drives between the sexes. For this reason the female genitals are referred to as *black hole*, *den*, or *half-moon*, while male genitals are referred to as *cock* or *bird*, images that express the outward movement of male urges, evoking not only the lowering of the testes, but also erection.

From there, the "broken window" takes on another dimension. Drunk and confronted by the moon, this man put his fist through the window pane in an attempt to repair an absence of maternal words for his own sexual organs. Inebriation brought back to life his childhood experience, while allowing him to no longer heed the orders of the moon—or his mother's words—that, in not naming the *little cock*, denied the existence of his own sexual organs. The movement of sending his fist through the window, breaking the pane, tried to repair this void by granting him the right to outwardly express his male urges. We can see the sexual symbolism hidden behind an act that appears symptomatic.

As for the child, contrary to what we like to believe in these cases, he was not disturbed because his father's drunkenness woke him up. Quite the contrary: having perceived the sexual symbolism with which his father struggled, the child became very interested with regards to his own need for identification. Glimpsing the coital symbolism without understanding it, he wanted to know more. That is why he declared that he could not sleep. "My window is going to break" was in itself a question that awkwardly summarized what he had understood and indicated that he wanted to know more. He was waiting for the complementary information from his father, and only from his father; otherwise he would have asked me. Moreover, he was skilled enough to get the answer by himself, and as soon as he got it, he quickly ran off to inform his mother: "I've got balls. Daddy said so!" In saying this, he affirmed that he now understood why little boys don't always behave themselves.

This example shows how *a lack of words concerning the "family jewels" can be transmitted from father to son through symptoms*. Without the words of an adult, a boy can neither imagine the solar strength of his testicles, nor can he touch upon the pride of his maleness. He cannot understand that when he reaches adulthood he will have a strength available to him that, like the sun, gives life. All he sees coming from his penis is urine. In order to understand this, the testicles need to have attention drawn to them in language. Isn't that what is meant when the testicles are referred to in slang as *clangers* or *clappers*?

Testicular eroticism and the relationship to money

Dreams, the imagination, and the unconscious frequently equate a man's liquid assets to his testicular production. The male genitals are referred to as *business*, *credentials*, *jewels*, associating the genitals with monetary value and the ability to work with the capacity to produce semen. These assets refer to the assets of the testicles as used in sexual commerce.

Moreover, our culture tends to judge a woman's morality by the use she makes of what the man produces in his testicles. The madonna and the whore are thus two antagonistic images that define how womanhood is perceived. On one hand, woman is an asexual image of the mother based on the model of the Virgin Mary, denying the need to use male testicular production. On the other hand, she is the image of the whore who, having sold herself to the devil, only uses the testicles in order to empty them for a vulgar profit.

Therefore, women cannot avoid the symbolism that associates money and the testicles any more than men can. The way in which a woman chooses to use a man's money depends on the way in which she uses, or does not use, his testicular production. When a couple has children and separates, the man frequently balks at paying alimony. He has trouble paying up, or settling accounts, not only in reference to his money, but also with regards to the relationship to his testicles. In order to regain possession of his testicles, he must deprive his ex-wife of the free use she previously had of them.

In listening to men, it seems that, in general, they do not understand the difficulty they have in taking on the responsibility of paying a living allowance after separation. This lack of comprehension originates in the fact that they are not questioning their relationship to their children, but protesting against their relationship to the woman. Whether or not they are separated, if the money that a man gives to a woman is not received as a product of his virility, he becomes a milk cow, with no guarantee that his wife differentiates him from her own parents. It is therefore difficult to admit that, after separation, she might continue to demand access to what he considers, unconsciously, to be equivalent to the product of his testicles.

In general, this type of conflict is no clearer for women than it is for men. They go for therapy either bragging that they never asked anything of the father of their children, thus denying that the children are a product of their father's testicles, or, inversely, fiercely claiming the right to continue to use his liquidity in denial of any separation. This is all the more striking when they have not had any children with him. The former husband becomes as asexual as a father, with the advantage of being less cumbersome because the woman places him in the nourishing role of a mother. These are women who unconsciously deny all sexual complementarity in order to lose nothing of the comfort represented by a mother.

A comparison of what men and women say in therapy leaves the impression that they are not at all preoccupied with the same questions. Women, far more than men, seem to be attentive to passing on life, to the aging body and to the discomforts which signal that aging. In their family and professional activities, they complain of being overburdened, of doing too much. The same goes for their love relationships with men. They are always fearful of having said too much or having done too much, of being too spontaneous or too indecent. Men's preoccupations are exactly the opposite. If they complain, it is because they have the impression of not having done enough. If they are ill, they are above all preoccupied by their profession. If they are in love, they anguish over everything that they have not done. They fear not having given enough pleasure or not having said enough. Be it in work or love, they always have the impression of not having done enough.

This fundamental difference in men's and women's complaints corresponds to a difference in their biological functioning. On one level, the way in which we think of ourselves and behave echoes the life of our body and our organs. This being the case, the oppositions between men and women stem from their anatomical differences. Producing and not producing are what differentiate the way the testicles and the ovaries function. A woman does not produce eggs. She functions according to the model of a bank. Born with a stock of eggs, the work of the ovaries is to allow the eggs to mature. Menopause thus corresponds to the bank closing. Men function very differently. All their life they produce sperm. A man liberates hundreds of millions with each ejaculation; this production is not subject to periodicity and has no time limit, which explains why women are much more attentive to their bodies wearing down than men, who instead seem to focus on questions of production.

In the conscious or unconscious image a man has of his body, the testicles symbolize creative power. They witness his virility. Testicle comes from the Latin *testis*, the witness. Yet they are also witness to the way a man experiences his capacity for work as an inexhaustible resource. The limitless dimension of his testicular production corresponds to a symbolism that presides over the pleasure of expending his work capacity. From this point of view, blowing one's pay in a single night can be considered a virile practice. For that matter, in 19th century British slang, *spend* meant ejaculate, and *spendings* referred to semen. Modern

French slang labels the testicles *les bourses*, meaning purse or, to be more familiar, money bags. Spending is the recognition that a man's virility is inexhaustible, that ejaculation in no way diminishes his testicular production.

Wearing the pants means ensuring the liquid assets of the testicles, making spending part and parcel of male eroticism. In masculine economics, offering flowers or gems is linked to a self-assurance conferred by carrying the *family jewels*. The production of a usable liquidity is central to male imagination and functioning. Thus, male eroticism is a celebration during which the wealth of the testicles is generously spent. It is through lust or spending that man liberally dips into the inexhaustible generosity of his testicles.

5 Erotic Pleasure and Gender Differences

Woman's sexual pleasure

Admitting differences between the sexes is one thing; accepting and assuming their implications is quite another. A certain number of adult men who come for therapy show evidence of an oedipal maturation that did not allow them to own and be proud of their own gender identity. They do not necessarily want to be women or resort to fetishes to compensate for being male, and they appreciate the beauty of women's bodies, but their own appear vulgar and lacking all aesthetic value. They love women, but hesitate more than other men risking this love because it does not empower their own bodies and their own gender. Certain men, like the actor, Steve, who as a child was traumatized by his father's womanizing and sadism, need to meet women who restore their body and their person to them. Because these men were unable to idealize an adult man's sexuality during the oedipal stage, and no words allowed them to become proud of their

sex, as adults they experience difficulty donning their male identity. Others, quite to the contrary, display a phallic certitude that
seems to function independently of their relationship to femininity, which is the reproach made against machismo. These men
possess the faculty of getting an erection prior to the demand,
thus denying all desire other than the one directly connected to
their own genitals.

Eroticism requires a self-representation capable of standing as
a possible actor in another person's pleasure. A man's fantasies
must bolster a desire to penetrate; a woman's fantasies, to be penetrated. But because he penetrates, we tend to consider a man's
pleasure as more external, less compromising, and more trivial
than a woman's, thus limiting it to a pleasure of conquering in
view of a single victory: ejaculation. The opposite sex frequently
responds obligingly to this attitude and thus favors a virility that
becomes inseparable from brutality. Characterized by the desire to
penetrate, to unearth an access to another person's body through
sex, male pleasure involves, if not rape fantasies, then at least
power fantasies that enhance the penis's value and reinforce its
capacity to conquer a woman's body. The male repertoire of fantasies always contains a possessive note, in that the penis must
appropriate the place where it will deposit its seed.

Nonetheless, the masculine position brings into play a man's
most inner facets. For men, as for women, sexual pleasure gives
access to the other person's deepest intimacy, but also to one's own.
Sexuality unveils images of the children we once were. This is, for
example, what sadomasochistic eroticism refuses to recognize.

Sadomasochism is a bastardized form of master/slave eroticism
that we will explore in more detail later on. Rape and possession
fantasies form the driving force behind this kind of sexuality, an
eroticism that enhances the value of phallic power and warrior
fantasies in order to guarantee that the territory of adult sexuality no longer belongs to the mother. In this kind of eroticism, we
see to what extent the child believed that the only difference

between his sexuality and an adult's lay in the fact that the adult could be freely sadistic. A child battered by the person upon whom he depends, the adult he idealizes, automatically reinterprets, in his fantasies, this violence as a pleasure that he gives the other. Reaching adulthood, he either becomes masochistic, only capable of continuing to consider himself a child in his sexuality, or sadistic, trying desperately to believe that he has finally acquired the real powers of adulthood.

We can now understand why sadomasochism reigns in sex shops. In seeking to transform the penis into an absolute master or an all-powerful weapon, sadomasochistic eroticism invests the penis with the responsibility of governing the somewhat frightening visions of sexuality that prevailed in childhood. By subjecting one's own internal child to a reign of phallic violence, one has the impression of mastering it, but in fact simply masks it behind cheap warrior representations. A sadomasochistic person carves a phony image of himself by trying obstinately to hold the penis's hardness and violence as solely responsible for sexual pleasure. Yet the intensity of erotic pleasure depends not only on virile qualities but also on the way the man's partner welcomes these qualities.

Of course men narcissistically center on their penises, but if they think they can only experience pleasure from their own phallicity, they may become envious of women, whom they view as the only ones capable of experiencing whole-body pleasure. At the same time, feminine pleasure is considered all the more mysterious because it is not linked to a specific organ. Freud himself saw female sexuality as a "dark continent," an area he was unable to explore. At the time, people wondered how women experienced pleasure. Did orgasm originate in the clitoris or the vagina? Clitoral pleasure was considered to be in continuity with the infantile pleasure the girl experienced with her mother, and vaginal pleasure a passage into adulthood, which explains why Princess Marie Bonaparte chose to have her clitoris removed when the psychoanalysis she did with Freud did not cure her frigidity.

In fact, men possess the ability to feel whole-body pleasure just as much as women do. Women are simply more at ease at feeling it and talking about it, not because a greater erogeny in the rest of the body compensates for the absence of a penis, but because femininity is characterized by the ability to welcome and receive, thus opening the doors to greater inner depths.

When a woman thinks about her femininity and talks about it to a therapist, she begins to unveil the mystery of her own pleasure when she approaches the subject of her own receptivity. Then she discovers her ability for whole-body pleasure, often a revelation for her. The pleasure she had felt to this point seems to have been eternally stuck in foreplay, because now she experiences the primal sensation of the energy transmitted through a man's penis invading her entire being, resonating throughout her cells.

Clearly, the notions of clitoral and vaginal pleasure do not suffice to describe a woman's pleasure: a pleasure which invades a woman's entire body eroticizing more than just the vagina. She considers the vagina to be a door that does—or does not—open onto a more global pleasure. Not limited to the clitoris or the vagina, this pleasure is transcendental for women, the only pleasure capable of profoundly reshuffling her unconscious body image and alleviating the weight she often bears from an identification with her mother.

In clarifying female pleasure, male pleasure becomes more mysterious. Does a man experience pleasure for the sole purpose of bringing his partner pleasure? Or can he experience a pleasure other than ejaculation that equals a woman's?

Man's sexual pleasure

Although concentrated in the penis, male pleasure cannot be limited to the conquest of a territory represented by the female body. It also resonates from a man's whole interiority. It too corresponds to opening the gates of his secret garden, gates normally closed. For him, as for her, sexual pleasure means delving into the very depths of his person, involving the totality of his body in a search for the energy, the internal forces, that convey pleasure.

Sexual pleasure corresponds to an intense energetic circulation resulting from mucous membrane contact. To arrive at this point, a man penetrates, and a woman lets herself be penetrated. But on the level of the mucous membranes, a man—just as much as his partner—involves the most intimate and profound aspects of himself in a reciprocal co-penetration of energies. From this perspective, the penis is hardly any more external than the vagina, because, above all, erection externalizes mucus membranes in order to allow reciprocal internal contact.

Why would a man's secret garden be any less fragile than a woman's? The difference in their fragility stems from their different relationships to the mother. While a woman realizes she has actually left her mother through her relationship to the penis and the resulting sexual pleasure, using his penis does not guarantee a man anything of the sort. Numerous and varied signposts crop up in his sexual experience, seemingly there to signal that in his sexuality he cannot elude the phantom of his own mother.

Enough men dream about having sex with their mothers to have allowed Freud to invent the Oedipus theory. This kind of dream, however, does not correspond to the transformation of pure and simple desire into images. The case of Don Juan demonstrated their primary objective: to mend childhood perceptions of parental sexuality. Although these dreams may arise frequently among men, a man's mother's femininity is not necessarily obvious to him.

Numerous men seek therapy for impotence after the birth of a first child. Generally, up to that point, they never encountered sexual inhibition with their wives. Only when they took on the responsibility of re-creating a mother did their virility find itself at an impasse. In this way, men discover to what extent their own mothers inhibited their sexual development by forbidding any representation of femininity in motherhood.

Other men who could pride themselves on the number of their partners seek therapy for another form of impotence that strangely arises when they fall in love. Loving a woman too much can lead to inhibited erectile abilities. These men often fantasize that their former debauchery will tarnish such a beautiful love. In this way, the representation of a mother who could never have been deflowered resurfaces through the women they love. As children deprived of the right to imagine their mothers as sexual beings, an image of the Virgin Mother hinders their eroticism. Loving a woman no longer as a plaything but as intensely as they loved their mothers transforms these men in bed into beings as asexual as the gift from God they had been for their mothers.

The simple fact of having loved his mother without ever being able to consider her in her own femininity is enough to make a man impotent. From this perspective, he is more fragile than his partner. Rarely does a woman's frigidity provoke suicide. Male impotence can.

By delivering her whole body to sexual pleasure, a woman transcends or goes beyond her identifications to her mother. She does not rediscover the one who, through her finery and clothing, had told her what was allowed and forbidden in the sexual arena. She rediscovers the one who, earlier and naked, carried her in her belly. That is why a woman's pleasure can resonate throughout her entire body into her very cells. No longer inhibited by references to images of the person who had been her mother, a woman's self-affirmation stems from an older identification with the uterus prior to birth.

Men function slightly differently. A man's sexuality also reaches its greatest dimension in the rediscovery of prenatal energies: in coitus, the penis's activity consciously or unconsciously replaces that of the fetus in the uterus, procuring a sensation of nirvana or loss of gravity. However, a man must transcend identifications concerning, first of all, his father's phallicity and the manner in which he as a child imagined his father sexually satis-fying his mother. In accepting the responsibility of experiencing sexual pleasure with his penis, he at the same time can repair the missing facets of his relationship to his mother.

If, as a child, his mother had not radically hidden from him that she was also a woman, the main burden in his love relation-ship to her would have been to put up with the immaturity of his penis and the impossibility of replacing his father in the maternal bed, which explains why sexual potency is one of the cornerstones of adult masculine narcissism. As soon as he uses his penis, a man guarantees that he has exited childhood. But as soon as he com-mits himself to a woman, he also may have to confront everything that was missing in his relationship with his own mother.

If his virility fails him, if his sex no longer appears as a giver of life and pleasure, a man can sink into an infantile depression, unable to do anything except project the image of a tyrannical mother onto any woman from whom he expects something. We can therefore understand why adult men sometimes indulge in promiscuity. Using their sex provides the first guarantee of their adult identity. Since the phantom of their mothers remains unavoidable in their sexuality, promiscuity protects men from having to rediscover the child inside. If a man only knows one women, he may confuse her with his mother. Inversely, if he can-not bear anything but multiple and superficial encounters that allow him to avoid the slightest relationship, he does so because it provides the simplest means to avoid rediscovering his mother in his sexuality.

Therefore, it is not in the depth of their secret gardens that men differ from women, but in the means of opening or closing the gates, a difference that develops during the oedipal stage. As soon as he can walk, a child can integrate the difference between the sexes. Standing up, he reconsiders anatomical differences because he sees them from an entirely different perspective. The power that a stream of urine acquires in its fall to the ground represents a new event. The ability to change its direction with the hands—like a hose—differentiates boys from girls.

The drives that ensure genitality structure themselves from this vertical stance. In psychology, *drive* designates an affective and sexual tendency, a life movement that acts as an intermediary between mind and body. Anal drives give form to matter, but also structure body form and the way we present our bodies to the world. They model excrements before expelling them. In a child's eyes, these drives have maternal connotations because they evoke the mother's body giving form to the fetus, modeling it before expelling it. Urethral drives, which push urine into the urethra and provoke urination, more radically evoke a masculine movement. Obviously, the strength of the stream brings to mind ejaculation. But for the child, and particularly for the little boy, it above all evokes the invisible manner through which a father identification provides mechanisms for sexual mobility, as we will see below.

This mobility, upon which adult sexual activity depends, differs greatly between girls and boys. One plays with dolls and the other revolvers during the oedipal stage. Let's not conclude that the "weaker sex" focuses on life, leaving the "stronger sex" a fascination for death. The little girl is perfectly capable of killing her doll. Death does not yet—for either girls or boys—have the irremediable meaning it will acquire with adulthood. For children of both sexes, killing is a game that enhances the value of life within a sexual mode that opposes life to death. For the unconscious mind, which considers death as the ultimate birth into unknown territory, killing equals giving life. But that does not explain the little boy's primary interest in playing with guns, which lies in being able to handle an object whose extraordinary power allows him to launch a projectile while maintaining control over its reach and direction. This new and improved hose, with an added projectile, foreshadows, far better than urine, the penis's adult modus operandi.

For children, as for adults, fantasies do not try to represent the penis and its functioning as they can be visually observed. Although a bullet or an arrow could evoke sperm, in general a child has not actually seen sperm. Even if he has been present at coitus, he couldn't have viewed very much, because the penis only unveils its force inside a vagina. Playing with guns represents an exteriorization and therefore plays a constructive role in developing male sexuality, for a man's sexuality directs itself outward, and a woman's inward.

Neither children's fantasies nor adult fantasies seek to represent the penis as it can be observed at a glance. If fantasies were to represent the penis as nothing more than a fleshy protuberance, they would provide no enlightenment about the force of sexual energy. Yet fabulous objects like weapons and musical instruments provide powerful metaphors for its activities and enhance its energetic force. Playing with guns primarily signals that a boy is preoccupied by the role the penis plays in his mother's sexuality. Feeling immature and incapable of satisfying her, he plays with guns in order to idealize the penis's adult functioning, turning his back on the infantile pleasure linking him to his mother.

Centered on the way the penis functions, virile drives enable a movement of emission aimed outside the body, a journey, possession, and conquest. Stemming from an inverse movement, feminine drives are polarized on the body's and the being's interiority. They enable receptivity, appeal, attraction, and the harboring nature of the uterus. Fantasies of attacking, penetrating, straddling, mastering and conquering correspond to virile drives. Fantasies of seducing, giving oneself, receiving the male organ, and letting oneself be conquered in one's deepest intimacy correspond to feminine drives. On this level, eroticism is intricately bound to warrior imagery for men, who perceive their sex as the main tool of their conquests, and for women, who, seeing in him a "tender enemy," endow men with irresistible weapons.

At the same time, men are far more preoccupied than women with the pleasure they are supposed to provide. As a therapist, you rarely hear women question their ability to give sexual pleasure. Men, on the contrary, are particularly worried as soon as they imagine, with reason or not, a weakness in this area. The common custom that delegates activity to virile drives and passivity to feminine drives only complicates matters. Whether they emit or receive, sexual drives are always active. Feminine or masculine, sexual drives stem from, above all else, a being's primordial generosity and the need to exchange with another person. Wanting a woman to be passive in her sexuality brings us back to traditional scenes that originated in nineteenth-century sexual rigidity. In numerous cultures, a mother plays the role of sexually educating her daughter in order to initiate her into understanding the way men function. In ours, we tend to educate girls by leading them to believe that when the time comes, they won't have anything else to do but open their legs. See no evil, hear no evil. . . .

Men, on the other hand, tend to consider themselves solely responsible for their own pleasure and for the pleasure they give. They therefore represent the vagina as a sort of glove, lacking any activity of its own, and cannot imagine that sexual pleasure can stem from anything other than their own erectile abilities. If, in penetrating a woman, a man feels little pleasure, or after penetrating he goes limp, he interprets it as a failure that is his alone.

Remember Joe's astonishment at the beginning of the book. After spending part of the night impotent with one woman, he discovers to his great surprise that he is not at all impotent with another. This leads him to conclude that there is no better aphrodisiac than a desirous woman. Until that moment, Joe had never realized the role femininity played in the quality of his erections. He considered himself solely responsible for all sexual pleasure. Afterwards I listened at great length to his rapture over vaginal vitality and the manner in which feminine energies determine the force of coitus. The vagina is no less active than the penis. The art of coitus involves both sides concentrating on the sensations and the fantasies that stem from desire in order for sexual energy to flow, and this energy accounts for the quality of the adventure. In this duo, the woman is no more passive than the man, and the magic of erection in no way lessens the activity that provokes it.

Male polygamy

The ability to satisfy many women at one time is part and parcel to male eroticism. Like in Fellini's 8½, a man easily imagines himself in the middle of a harem centered on his phallic ability, which in no way keeps him from also dreaming about a faultless monogamy with an ideal woman who is sister, mother, lover, and wife all at once. It is well known that men are more inclined towards polygamy than women. Very frequently women complain that men are womanizers. Women dream of being able to keep their spouse's penis on a leash. But they can hardly be ignorant of the fact that carrying out such a fantasy would have only one effect: to make their men go limp.

We can understand that, in a man's eyes, the harem fantasy could appear to be proof of his virility. But, more astonishing, observation shows that his polygamy also serves as proof of his virility in women's imagination and fantasies. Rare is the woman who does not suffer from an unfaithful companion. On the other hand, if in a couple the man admits that he was still a virgin before their encounter, the woman sometimes becomes sexually phobic of him. She then goes to see a therapist because this phobia, which makes her suddenly sexually reject the man she loves, seems irrational and absurd. Unable to interpret her companion's avowal as a lack of love in her regard, she doesn't understand what is happening.

On the other hand, when a woman avows virginity, and the man who loves her knows that he is the one and only person to have penetrated her, he generally considers it an erotic enhancement. In any case, he never interprets a woman's monogamy as a fault in her femininity. Men and women seem to view each other in different lights. While in masculine fantasies virginity is considered to have an erotic value that is all the more precious because rare, in feminine fantasies virile idealization of a man requires that he has had other adventures. This fundamental difference originates from another difference: that of oedipal structures.

The fantasies that animate sexuality are formed during the oedipal stage. This period begins when a boy discovers his hose and ends around the seventh year, the moment a child is initiated into social life through school. Common language makes no error concerning the end of the oedipal stage: it is called the age of reason because clearly a child can finally renounce the slightly crazy idea of marrying one or the other of his progenitors.

In adulthood, a person's oedipal structure translates into a personal range of fantasies that allow him or her to experience sexuality. This structure is different for men and women. The little boy models his sexuality in a desire for his mother; the little girl does the same in relationship to her father.

In the little girl's eyes, the boy has an advantage. With a hose, he possesses an object that allows him to differentiate himself from his mother right from the start. Visible, the penis appears to guarantee the boy's sexual identity. Not having one, the girl must find something else to make sure that she differentiates herself from where she emerged. Trying to build her own sexual identity, she integrates femininity through rivaling her mother. To remedy what she experiences as an anatomical gap, she has to seduce the man—her father—who, carrier of a penis, made children with her mother. A little girl's sexual development, and at the same time the health of her future femininity, thus requires a period in which it is possible for her to fantasize a sexual relationship with her father, which, of course, requires that she be able to perceive him as someone who satisfies her mother. This will release her, just like the boy, from having to satisfy her mother. Yet, although the father is the first object of her sexual desire in her childhood fantasies, the girl uses him only in a second position, because she takes him from her mother, which explains why, in feminine eroticism, the loved man is supposed to have known other women previously. The woman who becomes sexually phobic of her partner when she learns he was a virgin is simply running up against her own oedipal fantasies. Having dreamed as a child that she married her father, she could only have done so in her oedipal scenarios as a second wife, the first being her mother. Thus we understand why, in women's fantasies, the ideal man never shines with a virginal glow.

Female monogamy

In girls, the immaturity of the sexual organs does not necessarily inhibit development of fantasies enacting a sexual relationship with their fathers. A girl's genitals remain invisible, and she can imagine that they resemble her mother's.

A 4-year-old girl was brought to me because she had been regressing ever since her mother got pregnant with a second child. She refused to go to school, started to suck her thumb again, and acted like a baby. Her parents interpreted her behavior as jealousy with regard to the child they were awaiting. They were wrong. I questioned the girl in this direction, and a big smile signaled the joy she felt in seeing her family grow. I then asked her if something was happening in her own belly, and she stopped smiling, lowered her eyes, looked sad and shameful, mechanically going for the thumb and folding up on herself.

Here we were right in the middle of the symptom which worried her parents. I explained that she too would like it if her daddy made a baby with her, but it wasn't possible because her uterus was not yet ready. For a man to make a child with her, she would have to wait until she grew up like her mother. Her eyes opened wide with amazement. "Oh," she said. We made an appointment for the following week, and all the symptoms had disappeared. Out of her regression, she no longer needed to see me. Knowing that her uterus was immature, she could again idealize her mother and project herself into adulthood.

It is just as important to name the immaturity of a girl's uterus as it is to talk to a boy about the way his testicles function. The interiority of female genitals may, in fact, lead the little girl to believe that hers were mature like her mother's. A boy would not think in quite the same way. When he fantasizes a sexual relationship with his mother, he automatically runs into the visible immaturity of his sexual organs. His father produces semen, which preoccupies him because he is living proof of his father's testicular production, but he only sees urine coming from his own penis, obliging him to admit that he could not produce a child with his mother prior to reaching adulthood.

So boys and girls create very different idealizations of their fathers' sexual organs. In playing guns or transformers, the boy idealizes the adult workings of the sex he inherits. He thus idealizes the equipment that, in his eyes, differentiates an adult man from a boy. A little girl does not so much idealize her father's sex in its functioning as in the effects that she fantasizes it having on her body. Unlike boys, she is not preoccupied by the way the testicles function. She centers on the question of her own uterus. As one of the fundamental differences in their oedipal structures, this dissimilarity also explains why, come adulthood, men are, by nature, more polygamous and women more monogamous.

For a man, observing that his penis functions provides an important feeling of satisfaction in itself. The simple fact of having sexual relations reassures him, resolving the childhood questions about his sexual immaturity. So, differently from his companion, he can invest his narcissism solely in the activity of his sexual organs. It is easier for a man than it is for a woman to have sexual relations with someone he doesn't necessarily love. More inclined towards multiplicity in his sexuality, he is more easily satisfied than she is by a sexuality scattered among several partners because observing that his penis functions fits in continuity with his childhood idealization fantasizing the activity of his father's sex.

That is why men are much more vulnerable than women concerning the functioning of their genitals. If a man cannot satisfy a woman, or if he thinks he is impotent, he may be dramatically wounded. Being able to satisfy many, on the contrary, contributes to the narcissism of a strong and invulnerable penis in continuity with his childhood fantasies idealizing adult men. Men are therefore rarely wounded by promiscuity.

Promiscuity is more dangerous for women. They run the risk of being more easily disoriented when they opt for this kind of sexuality. A multiplicity of sexual partners can, of course, enhance the importance of a woman's sex, vulva, other parts of her body, or her attractiveness. She too is reassured she has reached adulthood. But, different from men, her promiscuity cannot ensue from the continuity of her oedipal fantasies and the fact that they were centered on the father. To remain in continuity with her oedipal structure, she cannot be satisfied with a sexuality that highlights only her vulva. The mystery of her own uterus being central to her oedipal scenarios, she has more need than her partner of being able to fantasize him as a possible progenitor, a man who she can link to the idealization she had of her father.

A woman's relationship to the penis is therefore very different from a man's. The oedipal stage turns them both away from centering on their mother by allowing them to direct their questions to their father's crotch. But while the boy idealizes the equipment, an activity, and a sexual functioning not yet available to him, the girl only idealizes her father's sex with reference to her uterus. Her idealization of the male sex does not relate to the pleasure she can get from it; the child is not aware of that pleasure. Her idealization concerns her father's capacity to produce babies.

In adulthood, a woman's tendency towards monogamy stems from the nature of this idealization. First of all, it is justified with regards to procreation. If she brings a child into the world, she must be able to tell the child who his or her father is, which could be difficult with a multitude of partners. Not being able to identify the father of her child can be, for a woman, a shame similar to—and just as painful as—a man's shame when he discovers impotence. This shame sends both of them back, each in their own way, to their childhood idealizations of the father. For a girl, the paternal penis serves as a cornerstone that allows her to build her femininity and to differentiate herself from her mother. Using the penis of a man she loves enough to procreate in order to bolster this foundation situates her in continuity with her childhood fantasies.

Much more than a man, a woman needs a reference to the penis that makes the person she loves unique. In bed, she is nevertheless surprised by the way her partner solicits her to talk about the pleasure he gives her. Neither of them is ignorant of the fact that all men are built the same and that the intensity of sexual pleasure cannot be attributed to only one of the two partners, but in love-making, a man may need to be told the contrary.

For women, the men they love are unique not only at the moment of coitus. Women are thus astonished that it is at this precise moment that men need to hear that they are unique. Women do not understand why they ask for so much verbalization of the pleasure they give. Why is it so important for them to know what she felt, when often she prefers to be quiet? When they try to find out if they were better in bed than another, women find them a little infantile. Women have trouble understanding that at that moment a man seeks proof of her love.

What keeps a couple together

The words spoken by a woman he loves convey a very definite erotic power for a man. Of course, they validate his phallic narcissism, but most of all they repair the area in which, as a child, he was forbidden to imagine his mother's femininity. The need to hear the words of the woman he holds in his arms is proportional to the way in which his own mother walled up all representations of her femininity behind the fortress of maternity. Invested in his own sexual power and the functioning of his organ, virile narcissism articulates itself around the way a man satisfies the other. In the encounter and foreplay, women ask men to signal their desire. In coitus, it is above all the man who needs to hear about that desire in order to rediscover the quality of the first stirrings he felt when faced with his mother. At the same time, when a couple stays together, rarely is the man responsible. Generally, the quality of feminine words keeps two people together.

Men are naturally inconstant in their sexuality; it is easy for them to change partners. Capable of satisfying many, it is rare for a man to deprive himself of something so intricately bound to the narcissism of his own gender. Feminine pleasure centers on the interiority of the body, the relationship with the being, and the hidden mysteries of the uterus. A man aims at conquering and fertilizing outside his body.

The fantasies of both sexes imagine virility as the capacity to occupy the greatest possible territory, which comes into play in men's social and warrior activities. Men fantasize their own sexual power in the same way. With his unlimited testicular production, a man goes easily from one bed to another. A man's fidelity is rarely responsible for a love story occurring. Femininity is not only much more active than masculinity in the choice that makes two people sexual partners, but maintaining the relationship also largely depends on the woman.

When a man puts an end to scattering his sexuality, when a woman stops him and a love story takes shape, it is because the woman singled him out, and because he is looked upon as someone unique and special, he settles on the person whose eyes fell upon him. We notice this when we listen to men talk about the choice of their companions. When they question themselves about the way they settled down with their partners, rarely do they have the impression of having chosen. They say that things just happened naturally because they always felt good with that particular woman. If they delve deeper, they notice that these feelings of well-being were closely connected to having felt chosen and understood, even though they had not yet considered choosing or settling down.

In the reality of sexual drives, the woman's so-called passivity is an absurd notion. Both partners are equally active in their sexual encounter. Aside from the Victorian ideologies that culminated in the nineteenth century, nothing justifies this point of view, were it not for the difficulty men have in seeing and recognizing that femininity is far more active than masculinity in the stability of love stories.

In the nineteenth century, women were far from obtaining the right to vote. Bourgeois ideologists sought support from religious institutions to justify their delirium over sex and masturbation. Let's not forget that these institutions went as far as asking whether or not to accord the right to have a soul to these penis-less beings. Since Adam was considered the son of God, they were only able to conceive of Eve as procreating at the price of a pact with the serpent. So nineteenth-century ideologists tended to consider that women, by their very nature, had a special relationship with the devil. "Hysteria" comes from "uterus." It was considered that these strange troubles came from the fact that demonic spirits resided, in a preferential manner, in women's uteruses. At the same time, Eve was judged far more lustful than her companion. These are the ideological foundations upon which the medical establishment proposed relieving young girls of that appendage—the clitoris—that was apparently useless to reproduction. In such a context, the feminine ideal was to have all appearances of passivity.

In our times, it is easier for men to recognize something that appears obvious to them as soon as they question the quality of the energies that activate their phallicity. Could it be anything other than the mysterious activity of femininity?

The questions our ancestors asked about the relationship between women and the devil stem from the very nature of feminine activity. That femininity can play a role in erection reveals the nature of its activity. Female sexual activity is less manifest than erection, which is inevitably visible. This imperceptible nature of feminine activity can render it enigmatic to men. When a man perceives and receives it, he senses an energy that is all the more invisible because it signals itself in him and in his body in a way—through his erections—that is, on the contrary, very visible. From this perspective, nineteenth-century ideologists suffered from the autonomy that characterizes the membrum virile.

Let's go back to the way in which the penis appears in language and fantasies as being separate from the man's body and endowed with a life of its own. It's called *Abraham, little soldier, Jack,* or *Dick.* It is also the *cerf-paon* of the dream at the beginning of the book, an extraordinary animal given to fabulous travels. This is one of the perspectives that, in fantasies, differentiates men from women. Experiencing his sex as a vehicle for pleasure and ecstasy, a man can hardly consider it one with his body. Erection is not subject to his own will. In his thoughts, it does not appear to be governed by his capacity for judgment and reason, but by this infantile and very personal language that is the dialect of fantasies.

In his fantasy language, a man is more united with his childhood idealization of his father's sex than with his own penis. Therefore, his questions about his own sexuality revolve around being unable to find a guarantee in his fantasies that his sex actually is one with his body.

In the dialogue with his penis, knowing what animates or inhibits this little appendage is the first of a man's questions. That is the question left without a response in the childhood of the sleeper who saw his sex as a *cerf-paon.* The dreamer addressed this question to his mother because it concerned, in a final analysis, the nature of the female energies that, like little snakes, animate his own penis.

Nineteenth-century ideologists suffered from this curious nature of female energies, which is hardly surprising for men who wonder about the dynamics of their sexual organs. When they noticed that feminine charms had the power to give their virile organ an autonomy contrary to reason, they said to themselves that their ancestors in the Middle Ages had been right to consider women witches.

The difference between the sexes can hardly be imagined devoid of any reference to the communication that animates sexuality. Although men and women differ in their essence and in their oedipal structures, nature nevertheless conceived of them in a relationship of energetic communication that makes them complementary in the act that unites them. By nature, man is emitter. His way of being mirrors the image of his sex. A woman also lives in the image of her sexuality. Her activity centers on the interiority of the body and the way her sexuality places her in a position of receiver.

The positions of emitter and receiver form the basis of loving eroticism. When a woman wants to seduce, she keeps herself from doing so in a masculine manner. She does not try to make a brilliant speech or brandish some kind of knowledge. She puts herself into a position to use her ears. She leaves men the privilege of words and brilliant ideas.

Permanently open to the outside, ears are feminine. On the contrary, words are emitted. They carry the same magic as erection. Like erection, they promise to make the world a bigger place. In eroticism, we experience words as a phallic equivalent. When a woman leaves a man the privilege of emitting words, he can think that he is the one who seduces. Blind to her activity that led him to speaking so well, the man takes a genuinely male initiative. It is no less his partner's feminine activity that is responsible for the pleasure he has in his own verbal activity. And isn't that already the beginning of love-making?

Opening her ears, the woman remains in continuity with her oedipal structure because by listening she can skillfully lead a man to recount all the adventures that preceded their encounter. That is why, even when she has children with him, it is rare that she really reproaches his polygamy.

One of the most common cases is the wife who seeks therapy because her husband is struck with a case of middle-aged lust. She comes in crying. She knows she is hysterical, but takes her therapist as a witness. Isn't it normal to be in this state after what's happened to her? "Can you imagine, she could be our daughter! . . . If at least he'd chosen someone my age!" "No," says her therapist, "it is precisely because she is your daughter's age that you've come to talk to me."

In response, she identifies with her daughter, remembering all the childish things she acted out as a teenager to excite her father. She doesn't know how he managed to resist her. She takes out a Kleenex and ponders this with a smile. Then she remembers she is a mother. Absorbed by her thoughts, she becomes quiet and gloomy. A slight inner smile brings her back to words. "Obviously, I prefer to see him sleep with that woman rather than with his daughter." This makes her laugh outright. Having dried her tears, she no longer knows why she is there. She finds herself somewhat useless, having bothered a therapist for so little. She would have been better off going to a museum or visiting a friend. She goes on for a long time about how much respect she has for therapists, but now she knows what she has to do. She pays and leaves.

Where does she go? Probably to a museum, because the therapist never sees her again, having nevertheless learned from her that sometimes a therapist's job strangely resembles marriage counseling.

6 Adolescence and Sexual Freedom

The imaginary murder of one's parents and becoming an active member of society

Many people describe how, when they reached puberty, sexuality—and particularly its underlying questions—fell upon them from nowhere, striking them unexpectedly like lightning. Human sexuality is strange that way: extremely present in children under 8, the questions it raises are then forgotten until adolescence, when they resurface in exactly the same form they had when abandoned at the end of infancy. This makes adolescence a time of great fragility. Transgression, mental turmoil, and the first depressions resulting from unhappy love stories accompany the awakening of sexuality.

In our discussion of the inherent difficulties attached to genital activity, we will examine in more detail how the human psyche—and particularly human sexuality—is structured by two expanding movements, two primal and opposing vectors or planes: psychic *horizontality* and psychic *verticality*. The horizontal expansion of sexuality is spatial, corresponding to building one's own generation, linking sex to pleasure, to siblings and to peers. The vertical expansion is temporal, inscribing sex in a succession of generations, linking it to reproduction, parents, ascendants, and descendants. *Adolescence is the period in which we build our sexual horizontality, its relationship to pleasure and to the space of our own generation.* Sexuality cannot be viewed in its procreative dimension right from the start. Prior to being able to consider sex as a reproductive tool, one must first discover it as a tool for pleasure and communication, a discovery that cannot be made in the relationship to one's parents. Before we look at how groups of teenagers undertake the delimitation of this new space, the space belonging to their own generation, let's look at how difficult it can be for a teenager to take responsibility for the novelty of his desire.

Listening to teenagers is the best way to understand how frightening genital pleasure can be. Choosing to be sexually active not only means recognizing oneself as the sole master of one's own desire, it also means accepting—or refusing to accept—a power that can be experienced as more or less dangerous: the power to perpetuate life. In order to recognize oneself as solely responsible for the fulfillment of one's own desire, one first has to shed the child's skin. In order to do so, a child must be able to imaginarily kill his parents, removing them from the pedestal where they reigned as masters of desire. This is one of the difficulties encountered by teenagers. Taking responsibility and becoming an active member of society requires relinquishing all need for one's parents.

From this perspective, adolescence forms the final stage of a long birthing process, after which a person should be able to take full responsibility for his or her own life. It is hardly surprising that this final birth can be a rich as well as painful upheaval for both parents and teenagers. Considering one's parents as simple mortals, although hardly easy, is the teenager's first task. He must reject them in their role and function in order to remove them from the position in which they thought on his behalf. At the same time, he very often faces a crisis period, feeling submerged by death fantasies involving those closest to him.

At this age, the relationship to the parents is always problematic. In order to enter into a socially active life, a teenager needs help, but for the time being he often has few established relationships. His parents are generally the only people who can help him, but as soon as they do so, they instantaneously handicap him by depriving him of the possibility of severing his ties to them. Therapy can help teenagers break from this vicious circle. This period is so important that prominent psychoanalysts such as D. W. Winnicott and Françoise Dolto culminated their life works by addressing the question of adolescence. Teenagers often rediscover the freedom of children, their speed and clairvoyance, their ability to perceive and verbalize the truth, which is probably why teenagers are, like children under 7, the only patients really capable of using psychotherapists efficiently without remaining in therapy eternally.

With the increase in hormones, adolescence can be accompanied by telepathic faculties as long as the teenager has not yet channelled this new energy into sexual activity. Certain traditions recognize these faculties. Taoist priests call on the psychic abilities of teenagers in exorcisms or family healing rituals, or for communicating with the souls of the dead. The Catholic Church grants the role of altar boy to pure and virginal young teenagers. Yet, if not acknowledged, adolescent clairvoyance can give rise to difficulties.

A young boy not yet 15, Paul, asked to see me to talk about his dreams. He thought he dreamt nothing but premonitory dreams. He told me a certain number of them and, as a matter of fact, everything he had dreamed had come true. A recent dream in which his father died in a terrible car accident on his way to the airport preoccupied him, causing a lot of anxiety. He had never told anyone about his premonitions, and for several days the idea that his dream might come true had frightened him very much. Then, one night, his father came home exhausted and furious. He had wasted half the day going to pick up a client at the airport. "You see," Paul added, "everything I dream about comes true." I didn't understand what he was trying to tell me. "But your father isn't dead." "Of course not," he added with a big smile, "that's what I don't understand."

I questioned him about himself and his family. He still greatly idealized his father, as children do, which enabled me to explain to him that, in my opinion, his dream revealed the upheaval he felt about becoming an adult. In order to do so, he had to rid himself of the way in which he still lived much more through his father than through himself. Dreaming his parent's death didn't imply that he wished him harm. It quite simply signaled that he must necessarily lose his parents in order to be born into adulthood.

Contrary to what Freud implied, *death fantasies concerning the father do not announce questions about sexuality, but questions about death*. In fantasizing the father's death, a child does not seek either to eliminate him or to take his place, but tries to situate himself or herself in a succession of generations. Above all, fantasies concerning a parent's death allow a child to conceptualize his or her own death. By identifying with them, a child can integrate an awareness of where life's project comes to an end.

As is frequently the case when teenagers seek therapy, Paul had integrated sexuality during his oedipal stage, but had not been able to integrate the concept of death. The adolescent hormonal rush brings sexuality to the forefront and, at the same time, highlights questions of life and death. Sex becomes as omnipresent and unavoidable as it was during the oedipal stage, except that it is no longer something to simply think about and understand, but now is accompanied by the novelty of having to experience it through the body, of having to literally embody it. Yet assuming one's sexuality means assuming life by confronting death.

During childhood, when sexual fantasies are formed, sexuality remains primarily platonic. Sentiments and tenderness prevail over carnal acts. Adulthood requires assuming the contrary while allowing the fantasies that invite one to experience sexuality to remain in contact with feelings. Having neither a period or wet dreams, a child can be considered, to a certain extent, immortal in the biology of his or her body and, in any case, immortal in his way of being. For a child, death is an abstract concept whose seriousness can only be perceived through the fear that it provokes in adults. Because the relationship to death is structured, like sexuality, during the oedipal stage, this fear is inherited.

In his platonic sexuality, a child tends to live like an immortal. The first wet dream or the first menstruation considerably overturns this order of things. Whether the child was informed or not, whether the parents allowed thoughts about sexuality or not, in any case, the body signals its future and distant end. Concomitantly, sexual fantasies manifest themselves, putting an accent on the actual, carnal, bodily aspects of the sexual orifices. So the adolescent finds himself faced with mortality at the same time that he has to unbind himself from his parents and enter a socially active life. Therefore, frequently adolescents feel a greater need to talk about their death fantasies than about their sexual fantasies.

The death fantasies that assail a person at this age can, most of the time, be reduced to a single issue: the difficulty of being born to oneself caused by resistance to untying oneself from those whom one has loved the most up to this point. Killing—even in the imagination—those who gave us life is not a simple affair. Submerged by death fantasies that he doesn't understand, a teenager can turn them against himself instead of expressing them. He thus protects his parents, but that is when he begins to suffer, because he shackles his own destiny, impairing its fulfillment.

Luther, or the discovery of his own desire

Luther was 15 years old. His parents had named him after Martin
Luther King. He was the last of three siblings, and his two older
brothers were pursuing their studies brilliantly. He was still in
high school, and his poor grades upset his parents. Ashamed that
he was less brilliant than his brothers, and very depressed
because, unlike them, he was unable to satisfy his parents, Luther
viewed his last two years of high school as torture. He became
passive, lost all desire and all taste for life. That is when a friend
of the family suggested he see a therapist and talked to Luther's
father. Luther made an appointment to see me.

He seemed lifeless during his first appointment. His shoulders
slumped, his lips hung loose, he spoke very softly and was almost
inaudible. Nothing seemed to have ever interested him, not
school, not girls, not any of the activities his parents proposed for
him, not even food, which he only swallowed to make his parents
happy. They called him "dunce" in school. His tactlessness turned
half of his teachers against him. Since he didn't understand why
he provoked such aggressivity, he found no other solution than to
turn in on himself, but there too he was bored to death.

He recounted all that in a monotone voice as if he were talking about somebody else. Everything seemed vain and illusory to
him. He had never understood what interest other people had in
always being so active. Was there really nothing in this world that
interested him? There was one thing: acrobatics. The gym was
the only place he felt alive. He went twice a week and on week-
ends when he didn't have too much school work.

As a child, he wanted to be an acrobat. Later, he wanted to
train to join the circus, but his father refused, saying that it was-
n't with childishness that you became a man. Did he still want to
be an acrobat? Yes, but now it was too late. He had to become an
engineer or a lawyer, like one of his brothers.

And what did he want from me? He didn't have the slightest idea. But his eyes lit up when he talked about his father's friend who had given him my number. While talking to him, he had understood that this man had himself gotten over a difficulty with life that was as persistent as his own, which made it that much easier for me to explain to Luther that psychotherapy was paradoxical because you pay somebody in order to be able to yourself work on your own person. Therefore, he would need to pay me himself, either through his allowance, or through any of the numerous odd jobs you can do at his age. This is what he did, and he decided to come once a week.

The first three weeks he did nothing but repeat over and over again in the same monotone voice his inability to desire anything. All dialogue had become impossible with his father. The latter made him work every weekend so that he wouldn't be kicked out of school. Faced with his father, he wasn't able to do anything but remain obstinately mute, further hindering their relationship. During our fourth appointment, he announced to me—with that same emotionless voice—that since the last appointment he had attempted suicide. He tried to inject air into his veins in order to die of cerebral paralysis. After relentlessly stabbing at his wrist for a half an hour, he gave up. He spoke in an impersonal voice, as if he had not been a part of his act.

Had he already done similar things? Yes, one time six months earlier he had swallowed a half a jar of sleeping pills, but the dosage was too low. He simply woke up very cloudy and had convinced his parents he was coming down with the flu. This time, as the earlier time, he hadn't said a word to his parents about his suicidal urges. The shock would have been too much for his mother. What could be more horrible for a mother than to see her child nullify all the work she had accomplished to bring that child into the world? I had to talk to him.

I began by asking if he took me for a mother who needed to be protected because he had not talked to me previously about the wish to commit suicide. His eyes opened wide with astonishment. In his opinion, was it, or was it not, a symptom to be unable to talk to one's parents when one feels bad? He continued to stare with wide eyes, incapable of responding. Then I explained to him that if he could not talk to his parents about something as important to them as his life, it was because he was at an age when he needed to take possession of his own life and, at the same time, dispossess his parents of it. It was clear from his expression that nobody had ever suggested something that simple to him. I added that by trying to inject air into his veins, he didn't only run the risk of dying, but also of winding up in a wheelchair, which was a very simple way of never leaving his mother. So it was time he began to talk to me about his own desire and what he was going to do to fulfill it.

He tried to argue, saying that it was exactly what he was unable to do. Last weekend had convinced him. In order to have him prepare a written examination, his father spent two full days making him work. All he had to do was to learn a few things by heart. Sunday night, he thought he had absorbed what he needed to know, but Monday, during the test, he had forgotten everything. He wouldn't mind being an engineer or a lawyer, but it was clear he was good for nothing.

I responded that if had he told me he wanted to be a doctor or President of the United States, I would have believed him. But I couldn't believe he wanted to be an engineer or a lawyer. His brothers had chosen those paths, which therefore corresponded either to their desires or his father's desire, but not to his own. "But I never wanted to be anything but an acrobat." "OK," I said, "if that's what you want to do, tell me how you're going to do it."

Empowered by having heard me tell him he had the right to pursue his own desire, Luther began to consider it seriously. He wanted to be an acrobat and nothing else. He had to take responsibility for his decision. He already had rather solid connections among acrobats and other circus professionals. He found out about the classes he could take and planned a training program in which he would continue school by correspondence. But for that he needed money. Since he was able to pay me, he felt certain he could also pay for his classes. He started working and saving his money, told his grandparents, aunts, and uncles that he preferred cash instead of presents, and he sold some of his possessions. After a few months, he had saved enough money to be proud of. He arranged his departure. Vacation was coming up, and he had found a job with a small circus that was going on tour for the summer, not as an acrobat, but as a handyman. He wouldn't be paid, but would be fed. He could become familiar with circus life and work on his acrobatics. His departure was set for the beginning of June. He planned to leave a letter for his parents and to never see them again. On the same occasion, he announced that he would no longer be seeing me.

On several occasions, I had tried to get him to open a dialogue with his parents, which seemed impossible for him. Luther was able to begin taking his own desire seriously, but confronting his father to prove that his own point of view was well founded scared him more than anything else.

After he announced his departure, I told him that his project appeared coherent, but there was one detail to which he had to attend prior to leaving. He had to tell me what I would say to his father when, after his departure, his father called me. Luther knew that his father had a hard time admitting that a therapist could treat a teenager without feeling the need to meet his parents. It was only because his old friend vouched for me that he allowed it. If Luther disappeared, I would, without a doubt, be the first person his father would call. I could try to explain to him that my professional ethics forbade me from answering any questions, but that would be a very uncomfortable situation both for him and for me. That is why I wanted to know Luther's opinion on what I should say.

"But," he replied, "I don't want my parents to be in on it." "I know," I responded, "you don't pay a therapist for him to speak in your place. You pay a therapist to learn to recognize the importance of words yourself, and that is why I ask you the question." My words seemed to make him think. Our appointment was over.

He arrived at the next appointment completely transformed. It was spectacular. He seemed to have grown three inches, his shoulders were pulled back, his neck stood up straight. For the first time since the beginning of his therapy, Luther showed off a superb athletic body below a large smile. He had resolved everything. He had jumped in head first and talked to his father. He said to himself that after what he owed me, he couldn't just disappear and turn his father against me. He had considered the problem for a long time and gotten the opinion of his father's friend who had given him my address. That is what gave him the courage to confront his father. His father had been very impressed by the sum of money Luther had saved and by the seriousness with which he had organized his project. Luther explained to him that by continuing his studies by correspondence, he could always take them up again if he had made a mistake about his vocation as an acrobat. His father accepted. The following Monday, he stopped school, began working at the gym, and registered for correspondence courses.

I saw Luther another three or four times. Everything was going well, and he didn't seem to have anything to say to me. But since he had started therapy following the model of the long-term work that his father's friend had talked about, he continued to come. Then, one day, a question preoccupied him. Why is it that since he began his correspondence courses he could remember things easily? When he was in school, he had spent hours with his father trying to learn his schoolwork without ever remembering anything. Now, by correspondence, he learned quickly and was surprised at first that he did not forget things as quickly as he learned them. Could I explain this to him?

His question summarized so completely what was at stake in his work with me that I started to laugh. I explained that he was beginning to become aware of the power of his own desire. Now he could learn because it stemmed from his own desire, whereas before he couldn't because it was his father's desire.

At our next appointment, he had given serious thought to this extraordinary phenomenon of desire. But now that he was aware of it, did he have to keep seeing me? I told him that it was up to him to decide. Did he have the right to stop right away? If Luther wanted to, why not? He had never talked to me about sexuality. I took advantage of the situation to bring that up, adding that now that he knew what he wanted to do, this question would surface. He could, if he felt the need, contact me again whenever he wanted. Blushing, he stammered his thanks.

Teenagers in groups : building a generation

A teenager needs to be satisfied with himself before he will dare sexuality. He sees his body transform, a surprise he generally cannot talk about to anyone who is not his own age. The experience of those older than him can be of no use because he needs to confront this new phase in life on his own and with those of his own generation. That is why adolescence is, above all, a period for peer groups, a time when the activities of the peer group one has formed take priority over personal desires.

This period, in which the person prefers the group over his own individuality, forms a necessary step in sexual and emotional development. Adolescence does not provide direct and immediate access to adult sexuality. It is the final formative period for sexuality, and teenagers appear particularly free in their sexuality because they profoundly need this freedom in order to experience the novelty of their bodies and their arising desires.

At the very beginning of puberty, teenagers generally form single-sex peer groups. This period, which precedes the actual entry into sexuality, corresponds to a reinforcement of the images of one's own gender. Through single-sex—homosexual in the broad sense—bonding, peer groups momentarily remedy the panic caused by a hormonal increase. Girls and boys oppose each other. The group serves to forge not only the ideas that one will have from then on about one's own gender, but also the images that will be presented to the other camp.

At this age, neither boys nor girls know what to do with the novelty of the desires they feel in their bodies. Overwhelmed by the completely new idea of penetrating girls, boys hide their timidity by sticking together and strutting their maleness. They are not so much preoccupied by actual sexual acts with girls as by what they can say about it among themselves. They first must give themselves an idea about what they can do with a girl before risking to do it. The same goes for the girls, although the way they giggle every time they see a boy is a sign that they are already waiting for the boys to run them off into the bushes.

This young teenage girl giggle is very particular. It signals the ambivalence that fills them at the idea that a man could penetrate them. It also holds a complicity that, among themselves, homosexually bonds them to their mothers while simultaneously displaying the brand new desire that a man initiate them to a pleasure they know nothing about yet.

As for the boys, virile drives surface as a desire to penetrate and conquer a woman's body. The novelty of these drives lies in the power fantasies that highlight the penis. Yet, to be able to dare such an act, a boy must first consolidate his fantasies. That is why boys feel the need to group together in order to evoke the real or imaginary exploits destined by their new state.

These fantasies are necessary to establish manhood. They allow a teenage boy to definitively disengage himself from the pleasures he experienced with his mother. Taking responsibility for initiating sexuality equals dispossessing the mother of the power she held, up to this point, over the child's body. While girls are dreaming about Prince Charmings that arouse in them a sexuality other than the one they experienced with their mothers, boys easily see themselves as Superman, who never needed a mother in order to take advantage of his extraordinary power. That is what boys want to believe in their peer groups. They idealize virile values and turn away from anything that could possibly evoke the mother.

Very rapidly, the peer group becomes mixed. It's the period of the first parties, the first flirts, of appropriating the body and discovering its effects on the other sex. At this age, the teenager still continues to invest more energy into his peer group than into the intimate solitude of a love relationship. His group of friends is the only thing that seems to count for him. His parents don't see him anymore except for meals and when he comes home to sleep. He could even give the impression of avoiding them. In any case, his desires correspond to the ideals of his peer group. He gives value to everything the group does and rejects what the group judges old-fashioned and outdated. He adopts the group's language and clothing. He lets his hair grow, plasters it with hair cream, or colors it, depending on the latest style among those of his age. Creating a clothing style different from that of previous generations makes the passage into adulthood visible by affirming that this generation is different and separate from their parents. The same applies to music and dancing. In this way teenagers create a new space, the space that belongs to their own generation.

To be born into adulthood, a teenager must definitively accept the loss of his mother's body, which is not necessarily a simple task. Turning away from the person who until this point was at the center of all of the child's emotional processes cannot happen without the help of an intermediary. The peer group plays this role. In the same manner that the mother had until now served as an intermediary between the child and the world, the peer group becomes a surrogate body that allows the passage into adulthood.

Generally, the group represents a body enlarged to the dimensions of the social space. It is a social body that unconscious thought connects with the maternal or paternal body, but that is, above all, able to defend its own integrity. An army corps is the same thing, *corps* meaning "body." An army corps defends the borders of the motherland and the soldier forms part of this body in a manner that evokes the way in which he was carried by his mother—in her—when he was immature. The teenage peer group thus appears as a surrogate body substituting for the role the parents had played. In this way, it prefigures social insertion.

Although the peer group provides a substitute for the mother's body, one must bear in mind that a teenager does not reject his father, but rather displays a profound need for a father figure. Teenagers express the absence of a father figure through the phenomenon of gangs. In this case, instead of prefiguring social insertion, the peer group or gang turns to destroying the social order, precisely because there is no father to provide access to that social order.

Homosexuality and the man-to-man encounter

During adolescence, homosexuality should not only be considered normal but, to a certain extent, necessary. Such a statement may, of course, appear shocking. In our culture, male institutions such as organized religion and the military are nevertheless bound by a more or less unconscious homosexuality that is all the stronger because it passes unacknowledged. The carnal dimension of homosexuality is banished because it menaces the upkeep of these institutions, which was not always the case in cultures preceding our own. We know that in ancient Greece, homosexuality was considered one of the most delicate arts of love. It was also considered necessary for the psychic growth of adolescents. From a psychotherapeutic point of view, homosexuality must not be considered exclusively from a carnal perspective. *Platonic or carnal, above all we must consider the emotional dimension of homo-sexuality as necessary to an individual's sexual development.*

A teenager must apprehend the way his body functions, recognize his tastes and desires, their relationship to other people and to pleasure, in order to develop the faculty of communicating through his own sexuality. That is why adolescence requires a wide range of sexual freedom.

Teenagers often feel the need to experience the way their body functions with several partners. This way, they can recognize the differences they experience with different people and, at the same time, discover that sexual satisfaction stems from a special quality of communication that they establish with certain people. If they feel the need to experience homosexuality, it does not mean that they will necessarily settle on it. Certain teenagers need the experience, if only to avoid ending up obsessed by something taboo that in turn generates fascination. Often, they feel the need for this kind of experience in order to affirm, for themselves, that they are not homosexual because the experience wasn't satisfying.

It is particularly homosexuality's emotional and platonic dimension that is necessary for the construction of sexual horizontality and the pleasure of accepting one's own gender. The relationship with the other sex brings into play complementarity, but does not allow the construction of the ethical values belonging to one's own sex. This construction requires a certain homosexuality that can be found in adulthood in friendship, sports, clubs, or any activity that excludes women. The construction of male values does not stem from complementarity. On the contrary, it requires rivalry with others of the same sex whom we esteem, respect, or idealize. People therefore need to maintain same-sex emotional relationships. That is the role played by the peer group at the very beginning of puberty. It is necessary for building and maintaining the images that the boy has of his own gender.

The group of buddies may exclude women for a long time thereafter, which is one male characteristic in adulthood. Religion, the military, all forms of assemblies, teams, and clubs that exclude women are nothing more than a final culmination of this first social organization. While a woman can recreate the lost relationship to her mother's body in the relationship to her children, a man cannot, which is why men create clubs, teams, churches, and armies. He can recreate a mother through ejaculation, but from that point on, his own body is excluded from the process. His group of friends not only includes the activity of his body, but allows him to recognize himself as part of a social body more powerful than his single person.

The homosexuality that reigns in men's peer groups is a gregarious, group-oriented homosexuality and therefore necessarily platonic. This homosexuality that bonds the group differs greatly from the homosexuality between individual friends. Special friendships create and allow an intense emotional relationship different from those experienced in the family. Like the peer group, they offset the anxiety and the unknown represented by the other sex. They allow the person to confront his own newness through the mirror of a similar person whom he idealizes and upon whom he can project his own becoming. Gregarious homosexuality contributes to the social integration that must be assumed by each generation. While individual friendships can be platonic or carnal, gregarious homosexuality excludes the sexual dimension of bodily relations that would shake the group's stability. Homosexuality is nevertheless recognized and addressed in the form of jokes and puns that reveal how the group watches over each of its members' virility.

It is on this level that the group takes over the role of the mother. Among its members, sexuality is as present as it can be in the relationship to the mother, but it is also as radically excluded as it was with the mother in order to avoid bringing into question both the tranquillity of male friendship and the maternal function of the group. This maternal function appears clearly as soon as a member of the group "chickens out," gets depressed, or gets drunk. His friends then take care of him in a maternal mode in order to reaffirm together that they are beyond the age at which this kind of problem requires the presence of a mother.

The group's maternal role also provides a remedy for the fear that can grip a boy when faced with the images he is offered concerning his virility. These are primarily images of combat that convey the idea that he must know how to fight and must be able to kill his kind in times of war. The group allows the boy to feel stronger and to intimidate possible aggressors. With friends, he can learn to fight without risks. Within the group, he can admit his weaknesses and fears, while outside the group he tries to show a full-time image of courage. A boy can experience a need to measure his own strength against another. Masculine values in this case are those of individual combat, of a man-to-man encounter, friends only ensuring that the combat be equal and fair. This virile encounter can also take a collective form, giving rise to gang-to-gang encounters, whose civilized social form can be seen in team sports.

Virility requires rivalry for its construction. The images a boy has of his maleness are strongly linked to his fighting strength, to his ability to victoriously face an opponent. All the numerous slang terms that compare his sex to a weapon imply the same idea. There exist a whole series of "sword" terms for the penis including *bracmard*—18th century British slang from the French word for a straight broadsword—and *dagger*, both presenting virility as the ability to use a short but powerful object to penetrate the enemy's intimacy, the depths of his flesh.

The man-to-man encounter therefore carries sexual symbolism. In a homosexual situation, faced with an opposing dagger, or someone of his own sex whose physical and sexual energy appear greater than his own, a young man has two solutions: run away or face the encounter. Let's not go so far as to think that he really confuses his opponent's penis with a weapon that endangers him and legitimizes his fear. He himself has a penis and does not confuse the fantasies that arouse it with the object he has between his legs. If he accepts the encounter, it is nevertheless this range of fantasies that determine the pleasure or discomfort he expects to experience.

In this kind of encounter, he could, of course, want to experience in his own body a pleasure similar to the one felt by the other sex if he were to use his sexual organ. Since he has no other means of feeling the pleasure that the use of his organ gives to a woman, this desire could seem perfectly legitimate to a young man. If he accepts this desire, he will nevertheless have to adopt a feminine position and momentarily renounce an investment in his own virility.

If, on the contrary, he does not renounce his virility, homosexual warrior scenarios will exalt it. The one-to-one battle, the duel, the joust provide fantasy models for the male encounter. Faced with another male, a man must defend the territory represented by his own body, thoughts, or ideals like a fortified castle. Investing his own strength with the ability to keep his opponent at a distance, he chooses confrontation to protect his intimacy from a penetration by his opponents dagger that would, at the same time, unveil his feminine position. Such a choice involves a certain vigilance in the sphincters, which, in the fantasies, are areas through which the body can be penetrated.

Bodily and psychic territory resemble the economics of a country. In the global economics of this territory, the sphincters and, more generally, the orifices are border posts that ensure the management of what enters and leaves the territory. The orifices of perception filter the psychic and emotional information that feeds or disturbs the economy. The eye is equipped with a door that closes when desired: the eyelid. Orifices like the mouth and the anus, which manage the circulation of liquids and solids, are also equipped with doors. The sphincters close off access. The man-to-man encounter requires special attention to these border control orifices. When we say "seeing red" or "scared shitless," that is what we are talking about.

7 A Boy's Femininity: Sex and War

Virility and the Mother

Freud barely differentiated the Maternal from the Feminine. Moreover, he did not claim to elucidate the mystery of female sexuality, the "dark continent" of his theory. As a result, he could not correctly establish the relationship between the Masculine and the Feminine. The Maternal and the Feminine trigger diametrically opposing fantasies in men, which makes it difficult to approach male sexuality without wondering why representations of women occupy two such distinct realms in male fantasies. A man perceives a woman as mother or he perceives her as lover, but rarely the two at the same time. The Feminine embodies the witch whose power arouses his member, or the whore who becomes his mistress, initiating him in the erotic arts. Both witch and whore form the basis of his relationship to pleasure, while the Maternal provides the basis for his relationship to procreation and death.

In accepting paternity, a man leaves the realm in which plea-sure governs sex and enters the realm in which he assumes responsibility for its consequences. His desire to explore all of life's pleasures and to create, through sex, the space of his own generation opposes his desire to perpetuate life beyond his own existence. His relationship to pleasure and the awareness of his own death govern the two primary directions taken by his sexu-al desire. Even when a man becomes a father, images of feminin-ity continue to remind him of his sexuality, while those of mater-nity continue to inhibit his sexuality. He is thus pulled in two dis-tinct directions.

In his fantasies, a man cannot help being bothered by visions of the Mother. As assured as he may be of his own phallicity, he can in no way rival the erection of the all-powerful belly that gives birth and, mirroring his penis, is vested with the mystery of life. In his fantasies, he can only tolerate maternal images after having named his own desire for children and even then, as we have seen, he may still find himself facing an impasse in his sexuality.

On a small scale, ejaculation represents a birthing process whose primary role is to recreate a mother, but as soon as the act is consummated, a man faces the pointlessness of his own phallic activity. His companion's new state no longer calls on his ejacula-tions as the major form of ecstasy in their communion. He wit-nesses her experiencing another form of ecstasy, one inspired by her relationship with the fetus, and he may therefore face certain difficulties processing his partner's pregnancy.

As if to demonstrate their difficulties, some men gain weight, rivalling the belly that renders them useless. Others become excessively implicated in their social activities, only to arrive at the foot of the conjugal bed exhausted, still without any guaran-tee that they accomplished a task as colossal as the one witnessed by their wife's conspicuous belly. Others abstain from all sexual contact, fantasizing that their penis could harm the fetus.

Wanting to have children certainly forms an integral part of male desire, but it is less related to the relationship between the man and the woman than it is to the relationship that bonds the man to his own father, to his ancestors, and to the reality of death.

In fantasies and the unconscious mind, virility represents the capacity to have left one's mother, which explains why images of virility mingle so intricately with combat metaphors. Taking the risk of dying in battle is one of the ways a young man ensures that he no longer depends on his mother. In taking this risk, he gains full possession of the most precious thing she gave him: his life. He affirms that from now on, it is his to dispose of as he chooses. This explains why a soldier's future wife perceives him in the full glory of his virility upon his return from battle.

A woman—and this applies to all women—finds it intolerable when the man she loves is incapable of leaving his mother. Having children with him changes nothing because it is not as a mother that she is wounded, but as a woman. If her man remains dependent upon his mother, it means he has not established an actual male territory, leaving her unable to idealize his virility, and she suffers in her own femininity. If he is the father of her children, she suffers twice over because she is no longer able to regard him as a father who can be idealized.

Delimiting a territory by severing links with the mother forms the basis of virility in the fantasies of both sexes. When people say that the army is good for boys, they consciously or unconsciously refer to the formation of an actual masculine territory. When a man becomes a conscientious objector, he takes on another form of virility that guarantees the same thing. Fighting for one's ideas at the risk of one's comfort or one's life guarantees a virility totally independent of the mother. Masculinity invests itself in the capacity to build and defend a material territory as much as it does in the ability to defend a mental or spiritual territory. It is in the name of the same male identity that the priest and the soldier both radically turn their backs on the mother.

Priest or soldier

More radical than the soldier, the priest forbids himself from recreating a mother by renouncing his sexuality. Becoming father without having children, he opposes the mother by presenting himself as her complement. The soldier, on the contrary, develops a territorial relationship that highlights his phallicity. His is another way of presenting masculinity opposing the maternal in order to become its complement.

The priest renounces the mother in order to consecrate himself to heaven, to the immanence of the Father and to the domain of God. The soldier opposes the mother by participating in the larger body of the army corps. He thus remains in continuity with the teenager who viewed the peer group as a substitute for a maternal body. His activities tend to recreate a mother that opposes his own and delimits a male territory: it is the motherland, the only mother a soldier can actually refer to.

Unlike women, a man is unable to recreate the lost dimension of the relationship to his mother through his own body or in the relationship to a child, and therefore he has to find another area in which to invest his feminine identifications and transform them into virile symbols. Generally speaking, a man fears discovering the face of a beloved mother behind his own when he glances in the mirror. He tends to flee any bodily identification with the person who carried him. Unless, as a child, he was kept from idealizing his father's sex, as happened to Peter, he invests his own childhood femininity in love for his father, thus reinforcing his father's potency in his imagination.

This need to define a separate territory for his childhood femininity enables an adult man to invest his energy in priesthood or war. The priest upholds his childhood ideal of his father's sexuality by continuing to renounce his own. Seeking in heaven what he did not find in his father, he reinvests his childhood femininity in his relationship to God. The soldier also remains in a feminine position under his superior officers. He thus perpetuates a child's game in which fighting with his friends, he defended the idealization of his father. As a child, he swore his father was the strongest. As an adult, he continues to uphold this childhood idealization by providing himself with superiors. Thus a man builds an exclusively masculine territory in which maintaining the homosexual bond to the father allows him to transform his childhood femininity into virility.

This explains why warrior images are fundamental to virile eroticism and play an important role in the fantasies of both sexes. Children of both sexes frequently dream of being chased by an adult man bearing a knife, a dream that often takes the form of a repetitive nightmare. The child generally wakes up his parents in the middle of the night as if to question them. In recounting this nightmare, the child expects the adult to provide information about the mysteries of life, death, and sex. Moreover, as soon as the sexual symbolism of the dream is explained, the child stops waking up his or her parents and shifts calmly back to oedipal scenarios.

Come adulthood, the phallic and penetrating nudity of the warrior loses some of the mystery it held in the child's dreams. It nevertheless carries a strong erotic charge in fantasies. Sexual frolicking can sometimes provide glimpses of an entire panoply of military metaphors in which the brutality of the soldier's behavior carries sensual overtones. Why? Because *in fantasies, the warrior's territory provides one of the few confines that radically exclude the mother.* Throughout history, weapons of all kinds have served to evoke the penis. All erotic treatises make abundant use of warrior imagery because for both partners in the erotic confrontation, warrior fantasies exclude all presence of the Mother.

Although rooted in the fantasies of both sexes, warrior imagery nevertheless corresponds to a particularly male eroticism. The warrior identity has sexual connotations for men because it accounts for what appears mysterious in his own sexual development.

Witch or whore

Generally speaking, when a man considers his own personal growth, he cannot discern how he went from the child's feminine position to an adult man's virile position. Contrary to women, he cannot perceive any continuity with his mother in his sexuality. At best he succeeds his father, except that he had no carnal relationship with his father like the one he experienced as a baby with his mother. If he uses his father as a reference point for his own sexual development, he encounters a mystery: the platonic dimension of paternal love. Fantasizing a bodily relationship with the father is more taboo for a boy than for a girl and, as a result, the metamorphosis from an infantile femininity to a sexually active manhood always harbors mystery.

The Judeo-Christian tradition embodies this mystery in God's creation of Adam in his own image. No bodily relationship bonds Adam to his Creator. Taken from his rib, Eve has a bodily relationship to Adam, but he himself cannot have one with God because God is considered bodiless. Christianity sought to make this mystery more tangible by introducing the Holy Trinity. The equality of father and son and of what binds them—a necessarily platonic homosexuality that is represented by the Holy Spirit—parallels the mystery of a man's own sexual development. Christian thought therefore places the mystery of male sexuality in the invisible mechanics that make the Father, the Son, and the Holy Ghost the three facets of the divine mystery.

Western man thus perceives the enigma of his own sexual maturation—the metamorphosis that transforms him from infantile femininity into adult virility—in the father–son relationship, which is all the more homosexual because platonic, and all the more immaterial because their bond can only make sense, in his fantasies, through a relationship to the Word, to language, or to the Holy Ghost, unlike the father–daughter relationship, which allows fantasizing a carnal bond. Therefore, in contrast with his

Greek and Roman ancestors, the Christian man is particularly vigilant about keeping his own homosexuality platonic. Moreover, if the Catholic Church little by little ended up institutionalizing sexual abstinence for priests, it did so not so much to protect them from the uterus that the medieval exorcists considered a privileged lair for the devil, but more to engage them in a platonic homosexuality that becomes a pledge of faith when experienced in the relationship to God.

A man's love for his father is what more or less consciously allows him to establish his sexual identity and, in addition, opens up the possibility of procreation. The pleasure he experiences with his own children stems from rediscovering a platonic sexuality similar to the one he experienced with his father. Yet a man's sexual identity also encompasses a carnal dimension that the mother–son dyad, although a bodily relationship, inhibits because it excludes the phallus. What then allows a man to structure this carnal dimension? Not a mother's femininity, but more the femininity of witches and whores who hold the keys to the kingdom of pleasure and are necessary images for virile expression.

The whore is supposed to know all the techniques of sexual ecstasy but, in order to meet her, a man must first pass through a mother figure—a madam—or through a known criminal—the pimp. Poorly regarded by other women, the whore only dispenses of her charms under the authority of questionable characters. The witch represents the woman who understands the magic of love potions. She travels astride a broom at night when others are making love. This image reveals what men fear in the witch: in her nightly flights, does she possess, with her broom, a more powerful instrument than his own? Or can she accomplish feats with his member that are unknown to him?

Faced with these two figures of femininity, witch and whore, a boy has every reason to perceive his sex as a rather rudimentary tool. Were witches not burned by men? And hasn't the whore always served as an outlet for rejecting the mother, a rejection that could not be mentioned in church? If a man does not limit sex to procreation, then these two figures determine his masculinity: a desire to taste the potions or to be knowledgeable about all the techniques of sexual ecstasy.

During adolescence, the final step in a boy's sexual development consists of facing femininity and its power over erection. We have seen that a boy doesn't take this risk until he consolidates the images of his virility in his relationship with friends. When he explores his sexuality exclusively for pleasure, and not for reproduction, a boy never confides in his father. He fortifies his desires with his peers. His peer group therefore plays an important role in his sexual development. Being part of a group protects him both from the bewitching woman who could make him lose control and from the whore who could seduce him.

Confronted with the power of the woman who arouses his member and who could make him dependent, the boy possesses only one opposing force aside from God: his phallic warrior force, which is exactly what the peer group strengthens. This phallic force, with group support, can express itself in many ways. A young man often first confronts a prostitute with his male peer group. The whorehouse then becomes a site for phallic homosexuality, which, in a warrior mode, serves primarily to gratify the exploits of virility. The group may push the military model as far as gang rape, allowing the rapist to venerate, in a very macabre manner, the phallic power of his ancestors, as if he wanted to make the woman he traps in his net pay for the other women he saw bewitch his father. Whether or not he takes his sadism out on a prostitute, a minority, or a gay person, it is always kindled by a feminine representation. He has generally seen his father fall into the arms of a bewitching woman, and he holds it against that woman for having taken his father from him. In a group, the power of phallic homosexuality opposes the witch's power, renewing a man's right to choose a fatherlike leader.

Unable to reconstruct the loss of his mother's body in the relationship to a child, a man works around this loss through the group. However, he is not, as Freud suggested, a simple "group animal." Peer groups do not produce only gangs and delinquency. In adulthood, they produce clubs, professional associations, teams, political parties, and, with them, the entire masculine organization of the management of power. From this point of view, bankers, industrialists, and businessmen are modern warriors.

During adolescence, sexuality is as omnipresent in the male peer group as it was with the mother and at the same time necessarily set outside the group. We have seen how gregarious homosexuality, which ensures the cohesion of the group, substitutes for the role played by the mother's body. *At this age, the peer group substitutes for the maternal body, but as soon as it provides itself with a leader or takes the form of a political party, it becomes, for the man, a substitute for the father's body.* Throughout adulthood, this father-substitute continues to allow a man to be part of a larger group. The platonic homosexuality that binds a group of men reassures a man because it replaces the platonic homosexuality that reigned between him and his father. It allows him to reinvest the vertical father–son transmission—which, through the intermediary of the Holy Spirit, made them equals—into the horizontal expansion of his life. Gregarious homosexuality in adulthood is thus the platform for social integration.

Westerns and the homosexuality of guns

The gregarious homosexuality that cements organized religions and armies is not necessarily phallic. Phallic homosexuality can be found in westerns. It belongs to warriors. It is a homosexuality that in man-to-man confrontations and individual combat celebrates the building of virile drives through rivalry. The "tender enemy" of erotic battles obviously has no place in virile jousting. The warrior does not pity the man who falls on the field of honor any more than the banker sheds tears for the colleague who goes bankrupt, which does not, for that matter, keep him from honoring his enemy, even after killing him.

In times of peace, individual and team sports provide fine examples of phallic homosexuality at its best. Whether based on a combat model of one-to-one rivalry, or gregarious group-to-group confrontation, sports highlight and celebrate virile performance.

Among all the human organs and orifices, the membrum virile seems particularly unadapted to fit together with its own kind. In fantasies, it can only celebrate an encounter with its own kind in a manner similar to the infertile sexuality of the child who plays with toy guns: "I kill you, you fall, and we'll have a good time." The warrior seeks in his opponent a confirmation of his own phallic power, thus establishing an erotic situation that is expressed through death and forms the basis of the esteem he holds for his opponent. Fighting under different flags does not differentiate them in their nature since, to the contrary, they are both taking on a male destiny in the same way. Between them, death is not a problem; it is the basis of a freely consented game. That one of the two could disappear does nothing but reinforce the respect for the one who takes full responsibility for the consequences of his choices.

A warrior finds no interest in confronting a person he does not respect or considers inferior or weaker. Such an act requires no virile qualities. It is far more worthy—and therefore more pleasurable—to fight with someone one respects or appreciates, or whose strength one fears. An enemy's strength enhances one's own because in the long run, one's own virility depends upon it. The code of honor reinforces this dimension of phallic homosexuality. Duels and combat ideologies enhance it because honor, for the warrior, guarantees the uprightness of his phallicity. The same applies to the written and unwritten rules of sportsmanship governing both individual and team sports. This code of honor serves the same purpose: reaffirming the rectitude of phallic power.

A man could fear sexuality because he perceives it as a tool capable of projecting him beyond his own existence, beyond his own death. In erotic ecstasy, he feels his being detach from terrestrial gravity. When he ejaculates, he perceives his body projecting itself into a life that, in detaching itself from him, speaks to him of his own death. He can assume the responsibility of procreation because he perceives his sex as the only tool in his possession capable of bypassing or transcending death.

While girls attribute the power to transcend death to the witch or to the uterus, boys attribute it to the phallus. That is why they like to play cowboys and Indians. "You kill me, I fall, and we'll have a good time" is a game in which "having a good time" means pretending to be adult men and experiencing, through death, that which the uterus seems only to experience through life.

By choosing abstinence, a priest transcends sexuality in his relationship to God. He becomes father without having to go through a woman, which in turn allows him to guarantee the immortality of the father, of the God creator whose immanence he upholds. The soldier/warrior also upholds the immortality of the father. He does so by participating in the larger body represented by the group or the army. As soon as the group gives itself a leader, it becomes a substitute for a father's body. A soldier's death guarantees the immortality of the *Vaterland*, the fatherland, or the king.

The warrior is therefore far from disdaining life. Using his phallicity at the risk of losing it is, as much for him as for the celibate priest, the consecration of an ideal of immortality. Both rediscover the boyhood love for their fathers in a father that has been enlarged to the dimensions of adulthood.

The warrior does not value death. He takes responsibility for it, serving a necessary function. He confronts his own death only so others can avoid death. The code of honor guarantees the protection of women and children. But it is for himself, and only himself, that the warrior cultivates the ability to free himself from the fear of death. The death he risks in battle would lose all meaning if it did not back an ideal of life. He confronts it in the name of an ideal of transcendence that on a collective level, sacrifices a life for a higher cause and, on an individual level, associates virility with the capacity to conquer the fear of death.

At a time when nuclear weapons bring into question the traditional warrior image, Western culture values phallic homosexuality even more. It is the basis of westerns and of combat films. "Let's shoot at each other and lie down" ends with a third premise, just like in childhood games, ". . . and we'll finally find out something about God."

Men have always felt pleasure in confronting other men because, in their fantasies and imaginary structures, a greater confrontation is at stake. They never welcome a woman who wants to come between two men. Men don't make that mistake. When two friends come to fight, other men form a circle to encourage the confrontation.

The uniform in women's fantasies

Male eroticism is characterized by a desire to exert power over a woman's body by fantasizing it as a territory to be conquered. This distinctive feature of male drives concerns all men, but exists independently of the warrior images that may or may not arouse an individual's sexual fantasies.

Fantasies are not limited to pleasant imagery. A man forms the fantasies that serve as an interface for his relationship to combat, power, murder, and war during the oedipal stage. A boy's warrior identifications depend on his father, on the conscious or unconscious attitude that the latter adopted with regard to one or another of the latest bloody wars that devastated the planet. The unspoken presence of a grandfather or other distant male relative may also influence these fantasies. In any case, they are not structured in a relationship to women. As with everything that concerns death, they are linked to the ancestral male verticality a boy inherits.

Political involvement, activism, or taking up arms all involve the libido, but not a libido directed towards the other sex, instead one whose goal is to repair or uphold the ideal held by the father's virility in the child's eyes. It is a libido whose homosexual motivations are linked to ancestry, and in which men often find it difficult to situate themselves. As we saw with Don Juan, a multitude of ghosts can haunt ancestral heritage. Ancestral phantoms govern fighting, arrogance, and male violence much more than they govern sexuality. Moreover, from a male point of view, this aggressivity has nothing to do with women. It concerns only the conscious or unconscious platonic love that bonds a man to his father. Whether he dons a uniform or refuses to take that responsibility, a man finds nothing sexually exciting about considering himself a warrior.

On the other hand, an entirely different question arises when a man takes advantage of the imposing bearing conferred by his uniform in responding to the desires of the other sex. In this case, the soldier's image guarantees virility in women's fantasies. Men, who are only supposed to respond with erection, can hardly find anything serious in this game. Playing the game in no way lessens the solitude that links warrior images to homosexuality and death in male fantasies.

Whether a man suffers physically or shines in glory, a woman's attention is attracted to the soldier because he was able to experience this adventure without her. How could he bear the sexual abstinence? That is what intrigues her. He allows himself an experience exempt of her. His territory excludes her as a woman and therefore excites her desire. The subsequent physical intimacy and its battles unveil fantasy scenarios that, prior to that intimate encounter, had excluded her as a woman. A soldier's bawdy jokes then take on a different meaning, becoming a gift of sorts, because, in correlation to a soldier's necessary sexual abstinence, a woman can discern in them a place of her own.

A woman can, of course, use a man in uniform to enhance her own appearance-consciousness, which does not inconvenience the erotic code. The oneness of the uniform corresponds to the multiplicity of her own dress. And even if different men follow each other under the same uniform, she appreciates each one of them for the same uniformity. Men generally do not complain about being appreciated for the sameness of their sex.

The sexual fantasies that surround the handsome legionnaire display him in an arid desert, evoking the power and strength of wild animals. Imagined as a beast thirsty with desire, his uniform provides this wild, animalistic collection of fantasies with a human face.

Sailors evoke other fantasies promising extreme but ephemeral pleasures. The ocean is their domain, and it is hard to imagine them coming to land for anything other than satisfying their sexuality.

Women also fantasize about the professional activities and athletic qualities of firemen. Always ready to put out fires, women attribute them the same swiftness in calming the fires of desire. Women's fantasies depict firemen on duty as always ready to put the agility of their professional qualities to the service of women.

Policemen are apparently less eroticized, although they do appear frequently in women's dreams. In women who reproach themselves for their slight sexual appetite, policemen abruptly enter their dreams to remind them of the law of sexual difference and the law enforcer's right to subject them to his club. Images of policemen therefore provide privileged supports for rape fantasies.

A little girl dreamed about a bandit chasing her with a big knife. The severe watch of an adoring mother forbade her any questions about sexuality. Much later, as an adult, she tells her therapist that she only once glimpsed her father's penis. She remembers her horror. Now about 30 years old, she suffers from frigidity and her husband is complaining. She dreams of a police-man who breaks down her door with an axe and rapes her with a bizarre savagery. Her husband is present, astonished but an accomplice, smiling at the show. She wakes up with mixed feel-ings of horror and pleasure. Then she remembers her mother's frigidity. And her own? Soon her therapist will hear nothing more about it. This insight sufficed to resolve the problem.

The policeman represents the law more than he does sex. The masculinity he could evoke in women's fantasies corre-sponds to a paternal masculinity, akin to that of a judge or a priest, which means that the eroticism of women's police fan-tasies is based on transgression of the incest taboo. But when a woman unbuttons the law's starched uniform, she unexpected-ly discovers a virile man.

Men easily accept being accomplices in women's fantasies con-cerning their phallicity. If for this purpose they use military pomp or warrior artifices, they do so to pay homage to the representa-tions the other sex has of men's virility.

Erotic games only act out fantasies. Those who participate do not seek to actually fulfill a warrior's destiny in bed. In bed, a woman could play the vanquished enemy and a man the military tyrant, but the game is a parody. This parody is part of the plea-sure. In the role of defeated soldier, a woman thwarts the implaca-ble logic of a military destiny. The submission she parodies trans-forms a scene that elsewhere ends in death into pleasure. Nevertheless, the logic behind this kind of eroticism is linked to master/slave eroticism.

Sadomasochism and master/slave eroticism

At a time when bankers and businessmen represent the new war-riors, sadomasochism appears to be a surprisingly marketable eroticism. Sex shops display all the gadgets of the warrior parade. S&M flourishes in second-rate films that depict the SS as a pos-

sible model of virility. Playing on an inability to handle the relationship between sex and death, sadomasochism displays a crudeness that in the long run conveys nothing other than a degener-
ate version of master/slave eroticism. The fantasies that nourish
this kind of eroticism take root in a rather distant past, only making sense in relation to the historical period in which the victorious army enslaved the defeated enemy.

In antiquity, victorious soldiers adopted those they defeated,
making them slaves, integrating them into domestic, family, and
sexual life. The status of slave was reserved for those who were
unable to conquer their fear of death, thus relinquishing all right
to their virility in order to continue to live. The warrior knew
fully the destiny that awaited him if defeated. Upon the victory of
the Spanish invaders, Inca warriors threw themselves off high
cliffs while their wives strangled themselves with their braids.
Besieged by the Romans in the Massada fortress, Hebrew warriors
did the same. The warrior's ideal of "conquer or die" aspires to
the goal of depriving the enemy of one's life. At the same time,
those who became slaves were those who, unable to conquer their
fear of death, renounced the virile ideal that attributes phallicity
with the power to conquer all fear of death. The conqueror relegated the slave to the feminine position of wife or child.

Primarily a homosexual eroticism, master/slave erotic scenarios
place the person who accepts being the warrior's slave in a feminine and bisexual position of child. Depending upon his master's
desire, the slave may be penetrated sexually like a woman or,
since he has lost his own virility, he may relinquish his own wife
to his master's sexual demands. He may also be disciplined like a
child in order to accomplish what is required of his new status. In
any case, he accepts a child's position because the warrior gave
him back the life that he rightfully could have taken.

In sexual pleasure and fantasies, master/slave eroticism enacts
only the end of the story. It eliminates the bloody images of war,
acting out only the warrior's periods of rest. Bathed in the volup-

tuous music of victory, it venerates the triumph of phallicity over death. Phallic power accompanies the rebirth of the slave. Virility takes possession of the slave's body, associating celebration and sex upon the return from war, a return which reintegrates the warrior into the maternal body and the motherland. Master/slave eroticism generates sexual pleasure because it places the male organ in the position of master.

The master/slave duality in eroticism promises pleasure for both sides because it has only one basis: phallic victory. Whether one submits to the tyrannical dagger of the conqueror or quivers with the power conferred by the possession of the sword, the game aims at transforming the membrum virile into a fearsome and superior divinity that reigns as master of the territory.

Yet men and women do not benefit in the same manner from master/slave eroticism. For women, the position of vanquished enemy allows them to occupy a space in masculine territory, to hold the position of soldier from which they are normally excluded. The warrior's arms are fantasized as a power greater than the mother. Giving herself to her conqueror, a woman takes from her mother the body she had as a child.

However, men, authorizing themselves the contemplation of their own phallic power, rediscover infantile idealizations of the penis, the guns, missiles, or rockets that, like Aladdin's lamp, conferred on them the power to carry out their fantasies. But in bed they prefer military parodies to space travel because these parodies relieve them of the weight of a phallic homosexuality that, in making them men, summons them to be warriors.

Men do not, any more than women, confuse fantasies that display their sex as a lethal weapon with reality, although they have more difficulty escaping from this kind of fantasy. They feel obliged to uphold the cultural image given to their virility, even if it means verifying its reality on the battle field. Warrior identifications are fearsome because they make reference only to homosexuality and to death. Moreover, how can men make sense of their warrior identifications in a society whose technology has transformed all battle into lowly butchery? Accepted or rejected, warrior identifications generally weigh heavily on men. Men enjoy military parodies in bed not because they are nostalgic for the battlefield, but because this eroticism thwarts the logic of phallic homosexuality that inevitably leads to actual battle and death by replacing it with a situation in which virility is less dangerous.

The slave's role is to respond to the master's desire. The fetish gadgets—whips, handcuffs, gags—that the dominant partner may use are simply gadgets ensuring that erotic play remains play, symbolizing the warrior's return from battle, his period of rest.

Dominant or dominated, both partners enact fantasies that only become dangerous if considered reality. Loving the dagger that takes possession of his or her body, the slave takes on the responsibility of restoring illusion to fantasy. Bequeathing the virile member with a power similar to the gadgets that parody torture, the feminine partner has but to use her charms to bring to light that the dominant partner's phallic power is no more dangerous than the plastic gun he played with in childhood.

Promiscuity and autoeroticism

In warrior eroticism, a woman has a more certain guarantee of entering masculine territory than a man has of validating his own virility. If a man can arouse his sexuality only through warrior fantasies, it means he needs to exorcise a homosexual dimension of his sexuality through promiscuity. But faced with the other sex, he risks reveling in a form of phallic autoeroticism in which veneration of erection can mask all other realities.

All forms of promiscuity provide continuity with a man's oedipal structure, but warrior fantasies provide continuity with a homosexual dimension of his sexuality whose mechanisms generally escape his awareness. Even if his childhood family universe forbade him from fantasizing himself in a sexual relationship with his mother, it did not keep him from playing cops and robbers and thus acting out, in his infantile scenarios, a structuring of his sex linked only to homosexuality and to death. Come adulthood, homosexuality and death are in any case the most enigmatic representations a man has of his sexual identity. Promiscuity primarily serves to push away the homosexual nature of his death fantasies. We generally consider the soldier's sexuality from this perspective when we complacently tolerate his bawdy jokes.

Phallocracy originates in a homosexuality that is all the stronger because it is misunderstood. It can express itself through a passion for weapons just as it can through a passion for the other sex. It transforms virility into an obelisk from the apex of which a man measures the territory of his conquests. A Don Juan often suffers from his warrior identifications. As we have seen, he may suffer from having a father who was dramatically wounded in his own phallicity. But when a man suffers because of his father, the suffering arises primarily because the latter never bothered to recognize his son as a man in the making. This lack of acknowledgement of his son's future manhood damages the son in the feminine, passive position he has as a child.

Another one of my patients had a mother who was very promiscuous. She was intelligent and did not tolerate that a man obtain her favors without considering that she also had a son. The child had been showered with gifts from an impressive number of "stepfathers," all very well known in the world of art, politics, or business. But none of these men had ever looked at him as anything other than a pet whose whims they needed to satisfy in order to reach their goal. Each time he arrived, armed with his childhood femininity, seeking in one of them a father even the slightest bit trustworthy, he was rejected like a burdensome animal. As an adult, his fantasies were full of animals. Very promiscuous, he viewed women as dangerous lionesses he had to tame or as healthy mares he rode with a riding crop. Repeating the way he had seduced and been rejected in his childhood femininity, his

only sexual passion was to seduce all the Sleeping Beauties of creation and then reject them violently as soon as they opened their
eyes to him.

For men, promiscuity primarily highlights their own phallic
strength. Promiscuity calls on femininity exclusively as an asset to
virility, therefore not necessarily bringing a man into contact with
an actual feminine territory. Let's not conclude that a promiscuous man doesn't like women. However, he cannot appreciate the
difference of one individual woman because he dreads rediscovering, in her emotions, the horror with which he experienced his
own childhood femininity.

A man can only become attached to one particular woman
through his own childhood femininity. Adults develop the capacity to understand the way the other sex functions because human
beings are, above all, bisexual. When a man is attracted to a
woman, he projects onto her a missing part of his own being: the
infantile femininity that his male identity did not allow him to
develop. He will appreciate a certain kind of femininity because
he perceives in it the qualities that he, as a child, attributed to
femaleness without being able to develop those charms himself.
He rediscovers in the woman he loves the part of himself that was
unable to satisfy his father, but this can only occur if his father did
not do violence to his childhood femininity.

*A man's relationship to femininity depends on the way his own
father considered him in his childhood femininity.* A boy's femininity
corresponds to a period of transformation during which he takes
the father as a model. If a father accepts his son's transient state
of femininity, the son dons a femininity from which he separates
at adolescence. Inversely, if the father considers it a lack of virility, he wounds his son, leaving him no alternative but to reject all
images of femininity. Promiscuous men were often wounded in
their childhood femininity and tend to continually be proving to
themselves the contrary. This phallic autoeroticism does not
exclude women, but excludes the possibility of identifying with

women. It overenhances the penis's function and could lead a man to use his penis mechanically like a weapon or a marionette, as Fellini illustrated in *Casanova*.

Of course, promiscuous men understand women, otherwise they would not know how to seduce them. But they take up erotic arms in order to avoid identifying with women. Sex soldiers, they venerate virility, but fear being unable to maintain its vitality on any battlefield. Running through endless battalions of "tender enemies," the women must disappear as soon as they are finished with them; the men confuse their childhood femininity with women's femininity, automatically obliging it to perish. So promiscuous men do not invest energy in women, but solely in the vitality of their own penis, which explains the relationship between womanizing and warrior eroticism. However, a promiscuous man does not use sex to exorcise the weight of phallic homosexuality that associates male identity with death; he uses it to exorcise all risk of once again finding himself in a feminine position.

Son of a soldier, the Don Juan of this book avoided his feminine identifications as much as he avoided his warrior identifications. He took advantage of both in his erotic scenarios, but only in order to respond to the fantasies of the other sex, or "to the strange but necessary ideas" needed for one or another of his conquests to reach orgasm.

Battling with skirts, donjuanesque eroticism displays a grotesque parody of the warrior because it primarily tries to evacuate fantasies that could evoke a homosexual aspect of a man's gender identity and a father–son relationship left unacknowledged in childhood. Don Juan incessantly told me that he never felt the slightest homosexual drive. However, he had no difficulty fantasizing me as a horrible castrator. Our relationship harbored that much more dread of the warrior's phallic homosexuality because Don Juan had never experienced the slightest structuring platonic homosexuality. He gave the impression that he had never expected anything at all from another man. He flaunted his virility, grasping onto it like a banner. But aside from the fact that he chose a male therapist, he remained totally ignorant of the initial relationship with his father and of the homosexual development of his male identity. He found these in his relationship to me, a relationship that highlighted the feminine images that had existed between him and his father.

Since his father had been reduced to the feminine position of an asexual man, until he met me Don Juan's fantasies focused on the image of such a man reduced to femininity. This image was capable of triggering great anxiety. I was myself seated and completely open with my ears. The feminine position of the Freudian father I represented contributed to drawing out his fantasies about my incapacity to contain his incestuous terrors.

Brandishing the horror of a sexual desire for his mother, he moved restlessly about on my couch like a fetus who might disintegrate into his own womb and the universe of his fantasies. It was clearly impossible for him to identify his sexuality with his father's.

His father's impotence forbade him from continuing to identify with him. At that time in his therapy, neither of us were aware of his father's impotence, but he was in the process of discovering it through his anxiety that I would be incapable of understanding his problem. Projecting onto me the feminine powerlessness of a castrated father, he tried to believe, with horror, that I was lacking all phallic means that could impede the incestuous violence of his own virility. Misunderstanding the resurging images of a masculine femininity between his father and himself, he avoided having to question the homosexual development of his maleness.

In one way or another, promiscuous men relegate all homosexual visions of the construction of their male identities to hell. They devalue warrior fantasies because they see nothing in them but carnival masks. Yet, unable to associate sex with death and with reproduction, they dread phallic homosexuality that much more because, like in a Molière play or a Mozart opera, they are in fact only waiting for one thing: the arrival of the Commander.

8 The Anus, Neurosis, and Virile Inhibition

Neurosis and the absence of desire

Neurosis is a dysfunction of sexual identity. Paralyzing anxiety, devastating guilt, or other forms of inhibition affecting one's life can accompany the idea of experiencing sexuality. Neurotic people generally do not know what to do about their affliction because they cannot localize it in their bodies. In fact, their suffering lies not in their bodies but in a failure in the fantasy structure that allows them to experience their sexuality. They are unable to envision sex as a simple tool for a communication that refines, transcends, or surpasses the use of words because they inherit their parents' way of associating sex with all the ills of this world. Confronted with their sexual desire, people suffering from neurosis produce a multitude of strange and persistent symptoms. With hysteria, mental or physical paralysis suppress all desire. With obsession, the obligation of accomplishing interminable rituals blocks all access to desire. These two major forms of neurosis reveal the extraordinary therapeutic effect of the spoken word. Psychotherapy is based on this astonishing observation: *neurotic symptoms arise in place of words about sex that cannot be pronounced, and these symptoms dissolve with the use of words.*

Both sexes can suffer from hysteria and obsession, the two major forms of sexual inhibition, or the two symptomatic sides of human bisexuality. Hysteria, a difficulty in feminine economics, appears more frequently and in a more demonstrative manner among women, while obsession, a difficulty in masculine economics, is more spectacular among men.

The obsessional man

Of all of the troubles associated with masculine identity, obsessional neurosis is one of the most surprising because it generates the strangest and most persistent immobility. This neurosis is characterized primarily by an inability to access one's own desires. As soon as a desire arises, obsessional men invent obligations and rituals of all kinds in order to divert themselves from their desire. Canceling out all possibility of encountering the unknown, they also annihilate all internal phallic aggressivity. In therapy, they are as punctual as clocks, never arriving five minutes in advance or five minutes late. They also never take the risk of missing a single appointment. They tend to use their therapists like a mother's breast, but do so with a militarylike punctuality and the respectful distance that one owes a divinity. Their fixity is stupefying.

In the overall economy of the body, the mouth represents the entrance, the In door. It manages the entry of material things, food and air, just as it manages all symbolic sexual and affective entries. A kiss resonates between the legs and presides over coitus. The anus, on the other hand, represents the Out door. It governs the exits. We may find it harder to conceive of the anus as an organ for emotional and sexual communication, yet as soon as a dispute arises, "Up yours" can be heard, quickly echoed by

"Kiss my ass." References to the anus thus serve as a support for a rejecting aggressiveness. A "pain in the ass" invades personal space. Similarly, when erotic fantasies include the anus, they concern the person's psychic limits.

An obsessional person's value system carries strong anal tonalities; it is a value system based on limits. An obsessional man systematically eliminates all disorder that could arise in his relationship with another person. All dirty or burdensome ideas must be rejected. He never risks treading on someone else's territory, not even in his thoughts. He thus excludes all possibility of being fertilized by a new thought. That is what renders him particularly stable, but also strangely immobile. The invisible limits he establishes make him seem unattainable, even by words.

Patients suffering from obsessional neurosis require delicate treatment. Questions of excrements and ownership seem to be central in their discourse, treading strangely on their sexual experience. We establish our relationships to the anus in our relationships to our mothers. The anus constitutes one of the body's psychic borders. As a result, we cannot help obsessional patients understand their outrageous reactions to excrements by referring to a father.

Freud recounts that one of his obsessional patients invariably paid him with carefully washed and ironed florin notes. It was a matter of conscience; he would not allow himself to hand anyone dirty bank notes infested with "dangerous bacteria" (Freud 1909). His sexuality consisted of masturbating young girls from good families on the sly. He had developed an ingenious system allowing him to end up in bed with them, but he nevertheless maintained a very strong sense of dignity and propriety that forbade him from compromising the girls' honor beyond these infantile games.

Accenting the anal dimension of his patient's fantasies, Freud associated masturbating the young girls with the cleanliness of the florin notes and asked, "But aren't you afraid of doing her

some harm, fiddling about in her genitals with your dirty hand?"
The man was so shocked that he cut off all contact with Freud.

There is often nothing worse for a patient than an interpreta-
tion that appears half true. It was true that the bills the man gave
Freud were to remain as immaculate as the young girls he spoke
of. Yet, by turning the question on him, Freud re-established the
context of the homosexual relationship his patient had with the
father he had come to consult. Confronting an obsessional man
up front with the question—unthinkable for him—of his homosexuality equals confronting him with the most insurmountable of
limits. Obsessional men suffer primarily from virile inhibition.
This one consulted Freud because he suffered from immobility in
his relationship with the young girls. Presenting him with the
ghost of homosexuality could only doubly immobilize him or
chase him away.

Obsessional men find homosexuality unimaginable because
the anus reminds them of nothing other than the mother. These
men often had mothers who took early possession of their rear
ends. Whether they abused suppositories or enemas, these mothers compensated for the taboo forbidding all contact with their
son's penis by an ever-so-maternal interest in his excrements. As
adults, obsessional men fear rediscovering with others the secrets
of their mothers' anal eroticism.

A newborn child does not master his anus. His sphincters are
immature. He must first of all mature physically and psychically
in order to be able to manage the closing and opening of this orifice. Prior to taking possession of it himself, a child experiences
his body as his mother's property. Potty training coincides with
the moment when a child can stand on the tip of his toes; he
takes possession of his body. But in order to do so, he must take it
from his mother. Observe children this age on any playground
and you will notice that they enjoy a favorite game when their
mothers call them: running away.

When a child reaches this stage, if his mother continues to stick her nose too frequently in his derrière, she will inhibit all his motor abilities. If she decides that enemas are necessary, she keeps him from taking possession of this part of his body. In his fantasies, the child will conclude that his behind serves to give his mother pleasure, and, as an adult, anything that reminds him of the anus will have an incestuous ring to it.

Anal pleasure and eroticism are intricately bound to bodily motor activity, to the pleasure of possessing one's own body and the other's body and to feeling actively responsible for the animal mobility of the body. In sexual fantasies, the pleasure of modeling, creating, rubbing, caressing, of driving one's partner or being driven, of harnessing, and of being ridden give sex its full animal and earthly force.

Blockages in anal drives express themselves through the incapacity to use one's body, which is striking in obsessional people. The rise of their own desire triggers a very particular panic. The simple idea of sexual intimacy disrupts their immobility. As a result, they use varied rituals to immobilize themselves again, allowing them to remain in a state of permanent hesitation when faced with their desires. They always hesitate between two things, never able to accomplish either one. "Maybe I'll call Martine . . . or maybe Julie," they say, spending hours incapable of picking up the phone.

This burdensome immobility that causes them to turn in circles originates in childhood. Even if their mothers had not dispossessed them of their anus at an early age, the toilet had certainly been the only place where they could find solitude, again relevant to the mother. In any case, they were children robbed of the possibility of playing. At the age when he mastered his sphincters, running away as soon as Mom called, an obsessional man was, in one way or another, held on a leash.

Playing is necessary for the development of the mind and the body. It contributes to mastering personal economy and prepares for the dynamics necessary in eroticism. An obsessional man's mother generally used her right over the child's body in order to forbid him from playing too far away from her apron strings. She justified her action by an exaggerated attention to his bowel movements, which could have been a useful way for her to avoid thinking about her relationship to an adult man. Like Peter's mother, she took meticulous care of her son, but instead of a fixation on his foreskin, her fixation was on his anus. She forbade him from being out too long, from playing in the street, from having friends, or from hanging around the "wrong kind" of kids; she was responsible for his health.

Generally speaking, she treated death as some sort of master far more powerful than the father. She cradled her child to the rhythm of a sad lullaby that showed him how, throughout the universe, the body becomes a corpse when weaned from the maternal goodness that gave him life. She harped on the death of children who preceded him, for whom she had never been able to mourn. Or perhaps it was the death of the men of her family, whose disappearance had definitively fettered her hopes in matters of love. Or she took him as her only confidant concerning the irremediable and terrible pain caused by the death of her own mother. In any case, she presented him a manly destiny unfortunately and inevitably bound to violence, war, and death. Thus she very concretely made it known to him that the slightest desire was subordinate to death, the almighty master. We can now understand why obsessional men suffer a fear of dissolving at the slightest quiver of desire.

Obsessional neurotics have their processes of desire short-circuited as children by being literally forced to orbit their mothers' bodies like satellites. Unable to bear that their children distance themselves to play, urinate, or undertake any other occupation, these mothers force their children to remain within view. Different from psychosis, this satelliting occurs at a distance sufficient enough to protect the children from incest, but insufficient for them to build the dynamics linked to an autonomous repertoire of fantasies modeled after the father. The obsessional man loves his father as much as he is ignorant of him, because his mother never presented his father as guaranteeing her own genitality. Her child's body, living and turning around her maternal apron, was the only guarantee of her genitality. This circular desire emerges again in adulthood in the very characteristic manner obsessional people have of turning in circles.

Unable, in his mother's sexual organization, to link his presence to the testicles of a progenitor, an obsessional man can maintain a multitude of secret relations with his father's ghost. He can encounter it in passing in the mirror when he seeks his own reflection. He can also call it up each time he thinks about masturbating. The idea of a corpse or a skeleton getting an erection is often central to his fantasies. A radical lack of fatherly words surfaces.

An obsessional man often perceives his father as a stranger. Long-term and silent company never really allowed them to get to know each other. An entire network of limits existed between them, forbidding the slightest intimacy. Death stood between him and his mother like a God far more powerful than the father. Thus, in his fantasies, an obsessional man often can only dream of meeting his father by invoking his father's corpse. This surrealistic and macabre fantasy world can be central to his sexual inhibitions. Like in the Victor Hugo poem in which the eye watched Cain from the bottom of the tomb, the father's eyes reflect his phallic inhibitions. They are either forbidding eyes that arise to immobilize the hand in its relationship to the penis, or, on the contrary, the fantasy of approving eyes that appear during love-making.

By invoking father and death as the two inseparable sides of the mystery that accounts for his sexual identity, an obsessional man maintains a strange relationship with his father: the collusion in his fantasies by which he subjugates the paternal reign to that of the corpse is precisely what keeps him from recognizing himself as the descendant of a lineage of men. He fantasizes so much about the vital presence of a dead father that he never meets the ghost of his grandfather. An obsessional man does not know that his father could have once been a child. He may implore his father's ghost but does so in the hope that it will guide him away from the unflagging circularity imprisoning his desire.

An obsessional man remains forever a mystery to women. He is as mysterious in the secret relationship that binds him to his father as he is in the accomplishment of the interminable rituals and heavy tasks that he must carry out. But he is particularly mysterious in his sexual inhibitions.

The tug between "maybe this one" and "maybe that one" reveals an obsessional man's paralyzing hesitations. The idea of having to chose between two women can immobilize him twice over. He doesn't upset his wife by taking a mistress, he exasperates her because he is no more capable of taking a mistress than he is of offering flowers to his wife. Stuck between two women, an obsessional man becomes stationary again, incapable of knowing where to address his phallicity. His hesitation between "maybe this one" and "maybe that one" leads him to turn in circles around the question. Without modifying the structure, he broadens the emotional territory that, as a child, put him into orbit around his mother's apron. As a matter of fact, he often only finds rest in the between-two-women state because "between two" provides him the only moment of solitude in which he feels he can exist for his own sake.

Men's obsessional anality can appear incomprehensible. One of my patients, herself a little hysterical, told me how she almost fainted when dining with an obsessional man. The man, rather refined and very cultivated, had been courting her for a long time. She had already talked to me about him, astonished that a man could need so much time before making his intentions known. He finally decided to invite her to dinner at his place. He lived alone in a small, impeccable flat. She felt ice cold when she sat down on a chair covered with transparent plastic. A drink warmed her up a bit, after which the man went into the kitchen. She offered to help, but he refused and she resigned herself to following him, glass in hand.

She was surprised to see him put on a pair of rubber gloves and a plastic apron. He had planned to serve steak with boiled vegetables, which, he had her notice, was a healthy and nutritious meal. Then she was fascinated by the way he manipulated the kitchen equipment. His gloves never once touched the food. He used a spoon and a strainer with a mechanical precision and a hygienic sense that reminded her more of an operating room than of a kitchen.

In a nonstick pan that seemed to come straight from the store, two steaks sizzled. He turned them with the tip of a fork. The meticulous attention he paid to them, and the hygienic sterility that emanated from every movement he made, provoked in her a very strange vision. She saw, in place of the two steaks, two sizzling turds. She gagged and, using the pretext of not feeling well, she couldn't eat anything all evening.

Sodomy

Generally speaking, there is something very male about the suffering experienced by obsessional men around their difficulty to master the workings of anal eroticism. Men do not like to have to account for that part of their bodies. In men's unconscious body image, the anus represents the only area they can imagine being penetrated, and it primarily evokes a less-than-perfect form of femininity. Women experience their anus differently. They can sublimate their infantile anality in pregnancy by giving form to a child's body. They can invest their energy in the gestation and expulsion of the fetus. Unable to do so, men can only sublimate their childhood anality in the possession of a woman's body. Their pleasure will then be to master it, to possess it, and to appropriate it as proof of their own power.

A need to sodomize thus tends to represent a sexual outlet that sails past the area where the obsessional man runs aground. But the pleasure that a man may feel from sodomizing his partner is also proportional to the way in which his mother precociously took possession of his anus. A child always fantasizes the abusive use of enemas or suppositories as a pleasure given to his or her mother. However, a boy will react differently than a girl because this enactment of coitus represented by the cannula or the suppository devalues his erections. In his fantasies, he tends to conclude that things happen this way because his mother must be depriving herself of the pleasure that he could give her by anally penetrating her. By turning around the situation in which he discovered this imperfect feminine pleasure that the anus characterizes for him, he rehabilitates his penis and the desire to penetrate. As an adult, he could rediscover this desire, intensely eroticized, in all real or imaginary situations evoking the relationship between the penis and the anus. We have seen that this kind of reversal characterizes the fantasy process. Sexual fantasies easily take the form of a denial because their primary function is to allow the subject to consider himself active in the other's pleasure.

The pleasures a woman can feel from being sodomized have the same roots. Just like the boy, she discovers the erogenous zones represented by the anus and the mouth in her relationship with her mother. The clitoris plays for her the same role as the penis for the boy. As babies, they both experience the same pleasure when being washed. In a girl's unconscious body image, the only orifice truly forbidden to her mother remains her vagina. Reinforced by images of prenuptial virginity, this taboo plays a primordial role in her sexual development, providing one of the pivots of her bodily autonomy.

The girl may feel frustrated that her mother's femininity cannot take her as an object of pleasure. However, this frustration allows her to understand that neither she nor her mother have a penis, but men do. In her fantasies, her mother cannot access the casket represented by the vagina, for which only men possess the key. Prince Charming thus holds the key to a pleasure that allows her to renounce the pleasure she, like a boy, experienced with her mother. Rejecting her mother, she turns her energy to men in her sexual fantasies. Of course, this process of sexual maturation implies that the mother can do without her daughter's body and does not use it to replace a pleasure that she no longer feels with her husband. If the mother pays exaggerated attention to her daughter's anus or clitoris, she inhibits the construction of fantasies that allow the girl to do without her mother later on. Precocious erotization of the anus provokes the same fixations in girls as it does in boys.

Nevertheless, women are less subject than men to obsessional neurosis. Women can more easily sublimate their anal drives in pregnancy and their obsessional tendencies in household activities. Maternal abuse of suppositories or cannulae burdens girls less than it does boys. For women, anal pleasure shares a status similar to clitoral pleasure. They are two forms of pleasure that remain in continuity with infantile pleasure. The pleasure of being penetrated through the anus rather than the vagina is particular in that it does not necessarily break with the pleasure experienced with the mother. But an exclusive fixation on the anus or the clitoris generally stems from an unconscious difficulty with severing from the mother.

One cannot compare the clitoris and the anus. Clitoral pleasure is independent of the penis, unlike anal pleasure. When a mother abuses her daughter, the daughter can fantasize her mother compensating for the sadness of not having a penis. From there, she could fantasize that a man sodomizes her in order to ensure that the penis is stronger than the mother. In this case, as an adult, her taste for sodomy will serve to remove her mother from the area her mother had taken possession of. The eroticism of sodomy manifests the uncontested master incarnated by the penis. In the mode of maternal omnipotence, this tyrannical master imposes his law and his desire over the girl's body *and* over the mother who may continue to lay claim to her rights over her daughter's body. But do a man and a woman whose sexual expression only vibrates the chords of anal and penile fantasies really distance themselves that much from the solitude in which the obsessional man stands immobile?

9 Problems of Adulthood and Procreation

Anxiety and guilt

The anxiety teenagers can experience in their struggle between the necessity to imaginarily kill their parents and the desire to follow in the footsteps of those same parents as active members of society and sexually active adults continues throughout their lives. Living out one's sexuality means admitting that one's parents are mortal, a rather difficult task for human beings. For that matter, neurosis witnesses the difficulties faced by the human mind resulting from severing from one's parents. In hysterical anxiety, a person anticipates and short circuits having to leave them, while in obsessional anxiety, a person incessantly confronts the impossibility of parting from them.

We have to sever from mother and father in order to assume the responsibility of having children, yet as soon as we procreate the model of parenthood that surfaces, in all likelihood, conforms to the model shaped by our parents. We can refuse this model or accept it. In any case, we would entertain illusions if we were to believe that the desire to procreate originates anywhere other than in our own childhood. While braving sexual desire requires an ability to imaginarily kill the parents, procreation necessitates an ability to question the role these parents played for us.

Sexuality flourishes differently from culture to culture, occupying different positions in the various civilizations that have appeared, and continue to appear, on this planet. Sexuality depends on the cultural values of the family and the society in which we are born. Therefore, we cannot consider genital sexuality independently of the moral and ethical rules we inherit from our lineage. Thus we see *the two contradictory movements that are at the origin of all the difficulties connected to genital sexuality: one that requires abandoning the father and mother, the other that requires the genealogical continuity provided by these parents.*

Sexual desire can provoke a variety of emotions. The mere idea of satisfying these desires can cause anxiety. Yet this anxiety is curiously proportional to the secrecy in which one has buried desire. Anxiety does not stem from fear of an actual danger. It signals a different kind of danger, linked to the fear of a potential encounter with the unknown, with a new territory or a pleasure foreign to one's usual system of representation and thought.

When provoked by sexual desire, anxiety signals the danger represented by an unknown erotic experience. In this case, the pleasure is obviously dangerous only on an imaginary level. When the potential experience of this pleasure triggers anxiety, this reaction aims not at protecting an individual from his or her own desire, but serves as a reminder that the price to pay for fulfilling this desire is the loss of one's parents. Anxiety therefore represents a latent awareness that in giving oneself over to the pleasures of sex, one radically abandons the first objects of one's love: one's parents.

But this truth is double-edged. Sexuality may provide the shortest and most certain path to the imaginary assassination of one's parents by its affirmation that one no longer needs them, but this in no way changes the fact that human nature is deeply ingrained with a reluctance to abandon father and mother.

Strangely, the majority of patients seeking therapy these days express the same difficulties. For the most part, they discovered masturbation with a sense of overriding guilt. However, only a minority of them had parents who actually repressed sexual acts. Masturbatory guilt exists independently of all repression. The guilt caused by using one's sex does not arise from the transgression of a taboo. It exists intrinsically in all children who are not informed that the laws of life and death destine children to leave their parents. While anxiety signals the loss stemming from the appropriation of a new erotic territory, guilt marks a resistance to dispossessing the parents of the property rights they had over our bodies.

From this perspective, highly sophisticated psychic mechanisms govern the tension that arises between abandoning the parents in sexual desire and facing the recurrence of their models in parenthood. In any case, genital sexuality, and particularly procreation, depend upon a balance between these two contradictory forces. We compensate for the necessary abandonment of our parents by the inevitable appropriation of our inherited genealogical continuity.

Pleasure and procreation

A person's psychic development, the foundation of his or her emotional structure and spiritual being, depends on the way the human mind develops during the first years of life and in turn, structures that person's sexual being. We have already seen that psychic development occurs in two apparently contradictory directions, on two primary planes that model the mind's complexity. One, the horizontal plane, enables the development of all the relationships that determine the space of one's own generation. The other, vertical, grounds a person in a temporal lineage and a cultural continuity.

Psychic horizontality links sex to brothers and sisters, to partners and friends, to pleasure and sensuality: everything that composes *the territory of one's own generation.* Psychic verticality links sex to parents and a *succession of generations,* to procreation, death, and the sacred: one's ancestral heritage.

Horizontality develops, first of all, in the relationship to the mother and, secondly, in all the activities that separate from her: games, sibling relations, and school friendships. In childhood, "playing doctor" does the trick. Coming out of childhood, the group of teenage friends, the gregarious friendship within the group, the first flirts, and the adoption of a new clothing style break from the preceding generation.

Verticality exists from the fetal stage, taking on a personal form during the oedipal stage. It develops through the child's relationship to his name, to his father, and to his ancestors, but also through the identification models proposed by his culture that nourish his ideals. In childhood, grandparents, godmothers, godfathers, guardian angels, or baby Jesus provide models. Later, a child identifies with heroes. A teenager will then choose activities that correspond to ideals creating a feeling of participation in the future of humanity.

The intersection of these two planes elucidate all the questions underlying sexuality. So while *horizontality links sex to pleasure and specifically to one's own generation, verticality links it to death and to relationships of lineage.* Horizontality requires a human being to be solely responsible for deciding the free use of his or her sex. Verticality integrates a person's sexuality into a succession of generations, between ascendants and descendants.

As a result, the Masculine and the Feminine have nothing in common with the Paternal and the Maternal. Masculinity and femininity stem from psychic horizontality, from sexual pleasure and erotic games. Paternity and maternity concern verticality and result from procreation.

Masculinity and femininity are qualities that structure an individual's inner sexual and gender dynamics. These qualities play a role in social relations and in the social image we choose for ourselves. The decision to become father or mother is an intimate, solitary decision. Masculinity and femininity provide the basis for erotic communication, for the pleasure of exploring life's mystery. Paternity and maternity also involve sexuality, but with the additional, new dimension of a platonic sexuality with the child.

One of the major difficulties faced in genital sexuality lies in the nature of the sexual relationship with the child, destined to remain platonic. That some religions consider sex only through its parental function pinpoints the problem. Father and Mother are vertical values. Having children, and particularly allowing the love for these children to remain platonic, is the most common way of preparing for that definitive end to all bodily pleasure that comes with death. But we flirt with catastrophe when we forget that the father's and mother's health depend, above all, on the man's and the woman's health, and therefore on the pleasure they experience exploring all the aspects of their bisexuality.

Child therapy illustrates this point well. Childhood psychosis does not arise because parents have poorly assumed their roles. Parents of psychotic children are not bad parents, as was once thought. They are parents who sacrifice their sexuality to their investment in their children. They invest their energy entirely in their children to the detriment of an adult sexuality that gradually becomes non-existent with the child's arrival. The children develop poorly or regress because these parents provide no adult representation of sexuality (Dumas 1985). One can therefore question the role played by medical and religious ideologies concerning relationships within the family.

While for a long time organized religions determined how parents explained sexuality to their children, today modern medicine plays this role. Yet, by considering the child only through his or her physical health, doctors systematically neglect that a child's mental health can depend upon that child's relationship to his or her father. That is what psychotic children teach us, for they experience themselves not as the product of a sexual act implicating the father's testicles, but as the product of the same mysterious alchemy bonding their mother to a priest or to a doctor.

In a children's hospital where I worked, when I asked psychotic children how, in their opinion, their mothers had made them, I systematically received one of two responses. The most common: "In the hospital." More rare: "At church." If I asked what role the father played, I always got the same response: "He earns money."

Limiting their role to financial provider, fathers fail to help their children. In the name of paternity, they no longer claim their adult sexuality and instead become spectators of a show that is often obscene: one in which their wives, in the company of their children, struggle with, or get pleasure from, the twists and turns of an infantile sexuality that denies the father any role. In the children's hospital, we observed that psychotic children often improved as soon as their parents rediscovered a sexuality that they had curiously renounced since the child's arrival (Dumas 1985).

Under the appearances of a platonic love, the parent–child relationship includes a sexual dimension that is not necessarily easy to deal with. The arrival of a child drastically modifies the sexual exchanges between two beings. A woman's mental health requires that maternity not destroy her femininity. We all know the facility with which mothers close themselves off in their relationship to their children, beginning a process of endless complaining. Forgetting that they were women before being mothers, their complaints focus on what they consider ingratitude—sexual ingratitude—when their children leave them behind for other activities. This mother–child relationship that substitutes for adult sexuality is not without consequences for the husbands.

As soon as a child takes form in the mother's uterus, it can perturb the father's sexuality. Numerous couples wrongly consider sexual intimacy harmful to the fetus. Men easily fantasize their sex as a dangerous object, capable of hurting the fetus or disturbing the symbiotic nirvana they imagine fetal existence to be. This commonly held opinion is entirely wrong. The fetus reacts to all the mother's stress, but also to everything that contributes to her health. A fetus communicates with the father through the mother's sexuality.

In addition, men frequently seek therapy after the birth of a first child because they have been unable to feel the slightest sexual arousal with their wives since the little one's arrival. Having recreated a mother, they have lost all contact with their partner's femininity. In paternity, they find themselves as asexual as Joseph was supposed to have been in Christian mythology. Yet, contrary to what could be believed, nothing weighs more heavily on a child than a father or a mother using the child's arrival as a pretense for renouncing his or her own sexuality.

In its horizontal function, sexuality is responsible for a person's mental and physical health. In its vertical function, it is responsible for another kind of health, the health of one's descendants, which we cannot contemplate independently of lineage. The complementarity of the Masculine and the Feminine thus governs an individual's health. The complementarity of the Paternal and the Maternal concerns family health, but only under the condition that, in becoming father or mother, one does not forget the man or the woman.

How a child creates a father and a mother

A child arrives immature into this world. His or her nervous system will not function fully until around the age of 3. Therefore, the construction of the psyche and the integration of sexuality depend directly upon the environment into which the child is born. We cannot conceive of the human mind nor of sexuality independently of the mother language that gives them form. The education we receive influences our sexuality right through adulthood. This continued influence can lead to real difficulties, although it is not necessarily pathogenic. It forms the basis of the morality and ethics that allow us to take responsibility for our sexuality. However, if we do not reconsider our inherited morality, it can generate diverse forms of sexual rigidity. In this respect, becoming father or mother is a test of truth, verifying our position with regard to this inherited morality.

During adolescence, we structure masculinity and femininity in the manner of our own generation, with our generation's own creativity. In order to leave father and mother behind, a teenager easily rejects learned morality. Procreation arises from a radically inverse movement, once again joining a person with his or her parents and situating that person in his or her lineage and ancestral verticality. In the process of becoming a mother or a father, one tends to rediscover the rigidity of one's learned morality.

The human mind does not obey the same laws when it evolves on the horizontal plane of its own generation and when it evolves on the vertical plane of ancestral continuity. We explore life's pleasure and sexuality with those our own age. We confront our own death with the arrival of a child. Paternal and maternal functions do not originate in masculinity and femininity. There is no continuity between erotic pleasure and the education of children. Only the arrival of a child creates a father and a mother; simply desiring children does not, because as long as the child does not yet exist, a person can experience nothing of fatherhood and motherhood. Paternity and maternity do not flow from virility and femininity, but are created by the child. Parents can then function in the roles created for them by the child because Father and Mother are, in the imagination and the psyche, entities that have existed for all eternity.

In fantasies, mother and father images allow a conceptualiza-
tion of the chronology of generations. These representations exist
independently of sexual identification. In dreams, father and
mother rarely appear endowed with sexual organs. They are symbolic representations, and because they are symbolic, they reveal
that parents conceive children with words, that we are only
human because we exist in a name. The mind is hard to grasp
outside the language in which it takes form. Yet this language
exists prior to birth and outlives death. Father and mother are
thus primarily symbolic images of the supremacy of language in
the succession of generations, which, for that matter, is how they
are venerated in the panoply of icons. God the father and the
Madonna have their counterparts in all religions.

Come adulthood, the idea we have of what a father and mother should be in no way depends on our own virility and our own
femininity. It depends on the parents we had, and also on our
grandparents and our ancestors. In our system of representations,
father and mother are timeless and vertical figures that govern
the survival of the community, of the ethnic group, and of the
species more than the survival of the individual. We find father
and mother figures in all religions because in the unconscious
mind, they symbolize a recognition of death more than a recognition of sex.

This perspective helps clarify one of the obscure points of
Freudian theory. Generally, we understand the Oedipus complex
as the belief that in order to reach sexual maturity, a child has to
eliminate one of the two parents in order to take his or her place
next to the other; thus summarizing slightly too rapidly a process
whose complexity depends precisely on the horizontal and vertical planes of the human psyche. On the horizontal plane, the
child's sexual maturation consists of fantasizing sexual activities
similar to those done by people of the child's same sex. On the
vertical plane, sexual maturation is more arduous, because the
child must conceptualize that these adults upon whom he is total-

ly dependent and whom he idealizes in his fantasies as his first sexual partners are, in fact, destined to die before him.

For example, in dreams one frequently assassinates one's mother and father. This dream is far too frequent to be considered a simple death wish, which would be a confusion between the categories of the conscious and the unconscious minds. While the conscious mind watches over a person's daily life, the unconscious governs life to a much greater extent. Depository of ancestral knowledge, it is not so much preoccupied with the person's survival as with his or her evolution. In order to do so, it places this evolution in the more global context of the family, the group and the species. For this reason, the unconscious mind treats death as commonplace. It presents death in dreams like an event lacking emotion and affect. With regards to the evolution of the species, death is nothing more than a banal event. At the same time, dreamed parental deaths express most clearly what one needs to lose in order to accept one's own evolution.

Therefore, in the unconscious mind, parental entities represent a psychic potential that exists prior to beliefs and religions, all the while justifying their basis. Father and mother are entities that govern psychic development and spiritual evolution. A child builds all his or her ideals through the images of the father and the mother. For that matter, his psychic development's dependency on the parents differentiates him from all other mammals. Throughout adulthood, these ideals persist in all the ways a person privileges the power of mind over matter and flesh, strength vis-à-vis death and certitude that life's movement will not end with one's own corpse. Father and mother therefore provide symbolic guarantees of the status of being human.

The little child, and afterwards the unconscious mind, haloes the parents with an idealization that renders them immortal. It is not enough that he create father and mother, he then bathes them in a divine light that transcends their mortality in order that he himself build a human ideal. With them, he learns the nature of life. He discovers sexuality, but also death. On the horizontal plane of his oedipal scenarios, he dreams of being of an age to experience his sexuality with his parents. On the vertical plane of the same scenarios, he is obliged to assassinate the divinities he saw in them in order to be able to imagine himself as their successor. Eternally present in unconscious structures, *father and mother are functions reborn with each child, but that perish with each adolescent.*

Conjugal life, pleasure, and philandering

Psychic verticality renders a man capable of sacrificing his own life for a group, a cause, or his descendants. Horizontality is not as subject to ideals. Masculinity and femininity emphasize an awareness of life more than a necessity to face death. Virility and femininity situate the body's aliveness and its pleasures in the space of one's own generation. Associating sex not with death and the sacred, but with pleasure and the relationship to the other, masculinity and femininity are responsible for reinventing life for oneself and with those one's own age. Sexuality is not learned from parents. It is reinvented with each generation, just like clothing styles, dances, and music. Aside from the role that the mother plays in the first years of life and in infant sexuality, horizontality is only shared with those one's own age.

Therefore, the nature of a human being's psychic inheritance differs on sexuality's horizontal and vertical planes. Sexual horizontality is first structured in the discovery of sensual pleasure and the relationship with the mother, and then through identification with the parents and other adults the parents' age. The child's oedipal scenarios frame the parents' sexual attitudes, which he compares to those of his friends and the people he frequents. In this way, the child carves for himself a place in one or another of the two gender polarities. The process of integration that orchestrates sexual dynamics excludes the grandparents, whom their grandchildren generally view as asexual beings.

The integration of sexual verticality occurs in an entirely different manner. On a paternal and a maternal level, the child's oedipal scenarios do not include models that he could have apprehended outside the family. On the other hand, they link his parents' model to their own parents and to their ancestors. The child thus places himself at the forefront of his lineage. While his parents and their friends help him to understand sexual mechanisms, his grandparents allow him, above all, to associate sexuality with death and the reason for his presence on earth.

Sexual horizontality and verticality thus correspond to two value scales that are not necessarily easily superimposed, but whose balance nevertheless determines one's genital health.

Sexual horizontality governs sexual dynamics, the exploration of one's body and of the other's body. All variations of pleasure, creativity, and promiscuity depend upon it. It engenders fashion and sexual stereotypes, machismo and feminism. It predominates in homosexuality, which privileges the gratuity of sex over reproduction. Above all, it is responsible for pleasure and emotional complementarity between two people.

Sexual verticality primarily sustains the awareness of the connection between sex and reproduction. It produces the majority of sexual taboos. It maintains morality and ethics. It generates the institution of marriage and nuptial rituals. It can be responsible for a religious vocation, but also for sterility. Becoming a nun or a priest, the mother or father of a church, without, for that matter, procreating unconsciously aims at healing the wounds of one's own parents. Sterility can use symptoms for the same purpose. In its essence, is sterility anything other than an impossibility to reproduce what our parents have done for us?

Genital sexuality can only flourish if one permanently straddles the horizontal and the vertical planes of sexual desire. All the bizarre aspects of fantasies are nothing more than the product of this first straddling between the desire to fulfill our parents, to lose nothing in the flesh relations that bound us to them, and the necessity of severing the bond and reclaiming our own bodies.

Celebrating the liberty and the right to use one's body, lingering over the mysteries of erotic communication, or exploring it with several partners are necessary paths to recognizing a certain solitude: the solitude of adulthood. Philandering distances a person from the family from which he emerges as much as from the family he recreates, forming an opposition by providing breathing space.

In these cases, society views men with more indulgence. We easily attribute them with sexual needs we qualify as physical, as if erotic communication could be considered independently of psychic processes. Apprehending things in this way primarily allows us to avoid dwelling on the nature and role of the psychic communication set into play by multiple-partner sex.

First of all, it is questionable to differentiate men and women in their sexual needs. In the cultural context that conditions their gender, men's sexuality differs from women's primarily by the divergence of their roles concerning the child. The mother participates much more than the father in the child's growing horizontality. She necessarily maintains bodily contact with the child, which implies sexuality. For this reason, she is automatically more pathogenic than the father as soon as she reduces her womanhood to nothing but its maternal expression. If she believes that her man has more physical needs than she does in sexual matters, more often than not she does not know that a mother's sexual abstinence primarily hinders the mental, emotional, and spiritual development of their child. When husbands make other arrangements, they reinforce this belief and rarely question the consequences for the child.

In our culture, we tend to oppose Virgin Mary and whore, as if multiple-partner sex were radically lacking in spiritual value. We cannot reduce validating one's virility or one's femininity in multiple relationships, or even with paid partners, to a mere physical or masturbatory act. Masturbation involves only virtual masculinity and virtual femininity, and does not separate from the parents. Having several partners risks that separation, and therefore does not lack emotional and spiritual value. It venerates, at least, the carnal complementarity of the masculine and the feminine. Just as radically as the convent, the army, or the seminary, it permits a person to free himself from the parental grip. It possesses a spiritual dimension because it allows a person to assume his or her bodily and psychic solitude.

We clearly see this dimension in the course of therapy when people who have been moderate in their sexuality momentarily engage in a promiscuous sexuality. In these cases, multiple partners allow them to explore the psychic potential connected to the solitude of their own desires. For that matter, great mystics often previously led libertine lifestyles. For example, in his youth, Ignatius of Loyola, founder of the Jesuits, was far more interested in weapons and women than in the presence of God. For that matter, one should not consider promiscuity a phase connected to the immaturity of youth. Its source does, in fact, lie in the sexual liberty required during adolescence for structuring masculinity and femininity. However, it is a necessary phase in a person's development that may recur at any time if it had been curtailed during adolescence.

The elderly are very sexually active in retirement homes, and even more so because at that age, as in adolescence, they feel free of the hindrances of reproduction. When we work with the elderly, we barely notice a difference between men's and women's sexual freedom, which provides proof that the parent–child relationship is the principle factor that can, during adulthood, influence differences of sexual availability between men and women.

Middle-age crises and their sexual explosions are not limited to men. They also occur among women, but are more closely dependent upon maternity. According to what they say, women rarely authorize themselves to take a lover during their maternity. However, they take one, often in a hasty and compulsive manner, when their youngest child reaches school age. Others wait until that child reaches puberty. They then consult a therapist in order to shrug off the stereotype of an indignant old lady. These women frequently had numerous children at a young age. It is moving to see them bringing into play an adolescence that maternity deprived them of too rapidly.

The necessity of validating one's femininity or one's virility can surge at any age. Promiscuity forms part of our culture because it stems from this necessity. It possesses a certain wealth because it turns its back on moral rigidity and on reason. However, maintained at any price, these erotic exchanges always occur to the detriment of words and the role words play in emotional balance.

In the erotic order of things, loving passion refuses to look truth in the face. Lovers easily allow themselves to believe that they could never part. This passion causes fear because it quite simply forgets that love also encompasses the capacity of losing the other.

A love ignorant of separation can lead to the tomb. Whether it be Romeo and Juliet or Tristan and Iseult, western models are very clear about this point. Loving passion can lead only to tragedy. Passion's trap lies primarily in the impossibility of losing one another. For that, it idealizes the loved one. It validates that person in passion's own dreams. It covers that person with passion's own secret desires. It also tends to clothe that person with a costume that only exists in fantasies. When these projections— through which the mirror of passion denies the reality of the actual people—become reciprocal, they can enrapture. Yet, taking into consideration only the reality of fantasies, passion's mirrors are deforming mirrors. Unfortunately, only catastrophe can shatter the illusion.

In more day-to-day situations, a person's narcissistic balance depends on the dynamics between virility and femininity. Sexual dynamics have an autonomous existence independent of parental functions. They exist prior to the arrival of the child and remain, independent of procreation, one of our major driving forces. Therefore, having children should change nothing in a couple's sexual dynamics. However, this is one of the most common difficulties encountered in genital sexuality. Numerous are those who complain that paternity or maternity treads on their sexual intimacy.

Contrary to preconceived ideas, procreation requires a certain vigilance in this interplay between the virile and the feminine. This vigilance has nothing superfluous to it because maternal and paternal do not exist outside the relationship with the child and, therefore, mother and father share no emotional dynamic outside this relationship. This is a major obstacle encountered in the status of father or of mother as soon as it overrides masculinity or femininity. We see this clearly in couples that separate after having children. Their major difficulty lies in having lost their emotional bond as men and women. As a result, they no longer know how to continue respecting each other as fathers and mothers of their children. This difficulty is all the more real because the children can in no way substitute for the sexual bond that was broken between their parents.

The child already has a weighty task vis-à-vis his parents. He creates the parental functions. In fact, he is the only one who makes those functions legitimate, because the father and mother exist only because of his arrival. In addition, we always forget that a child's first desire concerns nothing other than improving or healing the environment that welcomes him. We forget this because it seems too implausible that the source of all of a child's pathologies could possibly reside in the love the child has for his parents. However, this is what we were able to observe in the hospital for psychotic children where I ended up studying how children's diseases play a little known role in a child's psychic development (Dumas 1985).

It is particularly difficult for a child to admit that he cannot communicate with his parents through carnal acts. That is nevertheless what is at stake in his sexual maturation. During the course of this maturation process, he compensates for the discovery that he has no hold over his parents' virility and femininity by his ability to revive the affective exchanges between his parents and himself. We were able to observe that children's diseases often arise as if to signal to the parents a need for words like the father's words that resolved the insomnia of the child with the broken window (Dumas 1985). This does not mean that children's symptoms should be considered as emotional blackmail. It only means that children have that much less need for symptoms if they can talk to their parents about the contradictions they encounter between their desire to intimately satisfy their parents and the impossibility of doing so by the sexual means that bond the parents amongst themselves.

Children must recognize the existence of death in order to understand that they cannot marry their parents. On this level, children's diseases play a necessary role in psychic development. They allow a child to understand and integrate the body's mortality. It may appear strange that this awareness must pass through the body and through illness, but the reason is simple: all possibility of verbalization meets a dead end where death is concerned. Obliged to integrate all the universe holds, a child never stops asking questions. Yet regarding death, words always fall short. Parents never know how to respond to questions about death. If a child questions them about death, he automatically fails to make them react simply by using words. Illness is therefore necessary for him to be able to become aware of this limit that the existence of death places on the power of words.

We were also able to observe that child psychosis, and particularly autism, often go hand in hand with the absence of children's diseases. Parents of psychotic children are far from being bad parents. They are responsible for the fact that their child stalls in his psychic development not because they sin as parents, but because they accept being parents in a radical renunciation of all virile or feminine needs. Their libidinal and emotional dynamics depend entirely on the child who, as a result, has no reason to look to develop autonomously and to test this autonomy through illness.

We cannot encourage an autistic child to evolve without first of all allowing his or her mother to grant herself the right to a femininity that leaves the child a little to the side. But when, at the hospital, we achieved this result in the mother's therapy, we observed that the child then often emerged from his psychotic symptoms through a children's disease whose function was to renew a normal affectivity with his parents by signalling to them, for the first time, his mortality.

Since the child is already alone in making the status of father and mother legitimate, it becomes automatically pathogenic for him to be, in addition, something upon which his parents' sexuality depends. Adults unfortunately all too easily forget that a mother's femininity cannot, any more than a father's virility, depend upon her child. That does not mean that femininity must be excluded from the maternal role. Femininity is as necessary as a father playing with his child any game qualified as virile. Yet, using a child to argue for or against a separation is always very questionable. However, come the first quarrel, the majority of parents forget that they hinder their children's development by not being able to avoid using their children as a replacement for a sexual bond they can no longer find among themselves.

Becoming father or mother carries a certain danger to which we are rarely attentive. It tightens the relationship with one's spouse but, outside this single relationship, offers no emotional link to those of one's own age group. Men throw stag parties to bury their youthful ways. Women frequently bury their careers. Both risk seclusion with the arrival of children. We have just pinpointed the fragility of the parental status: mother and father are entities incapable of governing affective relations other than those of ascent and descent.

On the contrary, the force of virility and femininity resides in the fact that they turn their backs on the platonic relationships implied by family. This force that allows the teenager to leave his parents is the same that allows a couple to separate. The masculine and the feminine exist independently of the child and, moreover, are the only positions capable of situating a person in his or her activities among those of the same age group.

Reason and separation

Paternity and maternity depend upon masculinity and femininity, but the contrary is not true. Sexual pleasure and the desire to have children can only be linked if one accepts the rules of this dependence. In a couple, father and mother depend upon an interwoven relationship with man and woman that on one hand subjugates maternity to the masculinity of a man's testicular production, and on the other subjugates paternity to the femininity that designates the father, allowing the child to carry the father's name. Only under these conditions can genital sexuality blossom, balancing the desire to become father and mother and the desire to remain man and woman.

Maternity depends on virility because it results from virility. The status of mother is subject to a man's testicular production, as much as it is to his work capacity. On this level, a couple's health depends on the imaginary and symbolic value that the woman attributes to her man's *jewels*. Yet this is also the area in which phallic generosity opposes the omnipotent mother.

A man can only feel implicated in maternity if he feels responsible for it. If he is not the creator, or if it did not directly involve his sex, maternity inhibits a man because it reminds him of the period when he had been dependent upon his mother. Therefore a man has no choice but to resist a maternity that pretends to exist independently of his sex. If his partner no longer attributes his testicles with the creative power upon which the maternity depends, she renders him incapable of backing her as a mother.

Again, we have described one of the most frequent problems faced by couples who separate. A man equates monetary liquidity with his testicular liquidity and, as a result, finds it very difficult to put up with his wife continuing to use his wallet once they have separated. This question arises so frequently in relationships between men and women that we cannot reduce it to a simple economic problem. We must view it as a fundamental male protest that has some basis. The money that a man gives a women, even after separation, continues to symbolize his virility. Seen from the woman's perspective, the question of separation boils down to the same thing. Whether or not she is aware of it, a woman's relationship to a man centers on his testicular production. Even if she is a call girl and only interested in his money, the same thing is always at stake.

As mothers, women often seek therapy for their children when they have broken off all contact with the fathers. They proudly announce that, since their separation, they have refrained from depending upon the children's father or from asking for anything. Although this reaction may be rather healthy from the point of view of her own personal economy, it in no way takes into consideration the children's development.

A child needs his or her father in order to develop. A child needs him even if that father is dead, because the father influences a child's psychic development whether or not they live under the same roof. If the mother lives with another man, the child can, of course, build his sexual identity in identification with this man, but only on one condition: that his progenitor be respected by the man who replaces him. This explains the classic problem of the ferocious hatred a boy expresses for his stepfather. Men in the position of stepfathers should not forget that they will never occupy the slightest structuring position for a woman's children if their good intentions towards those children devalue the progenitor.

If a woman abstains from asking anything of the father of her children under the pretext that she has left him, her attitude is absurd from the point of view of the children's development. This attitude does not bring into question the vertical image of the original father since, in any case, the child carries an image of his father deep inside, be it only on an unconscious level. If the father refuses to give money to the mother, the child may judge him as stingy or selfish, but he will never doubt his father's virility. For that matter, isn't his refusal living proof of that virility? On the other hand, if the mother refuses the father's money, the child will view it as a fault in her femininity, a frailty that is hers alone, because the very fact of his own presence keeps him from understanding his mother's rejection of his father's phallic generosity.

We generally accept that the male role is to support the maternal beyond the simple festivities of love-making. It is also necessary to admit that femininity can have other functions than those related to the quality of the erection. Because of the child, masculinity owes it to itself to support maternity. For the same reason, femininity must support paternity. For this reason, refusing to accept anything from the father of one's child can only be understood, in the child's mind, as a fault in a mother's femininity.

Backing the maternal is so central to masculine imagination that it provides the framework for the soldier's value system. A young man does not run off to commit suicide in the arms of his mother country because of a first, unhappy love affair. In all cultures, virility ensures the integrity of the motherland. The warrior's code of ethics therefore engenders a code of honor that protects women and children. In the relationship to a moral code and an ancestral lineage, masculinity recognizes its essential role in guaranteeing the survival of the maternal.

The same applies to the relationship between femininity and paternity. Whatever a woman's relationship to men, she first of all

backs the father of her children and does so because of her oedipal structure. A boy's sexual maturation centers on the desire to
and the impossibility of fulfilling the mother. A girl's sexual maturation depends on a similar relationship to the father. Yet, in
adulthood, father and mother exist only in relationship to the
child. Only this new arrival justifies upholding these parental
images. In the child's development, the way in which femininity
upholds paternity plays a very different role than the one played
by virility recognizing the maternal as the result of its acts. Having
to safeguard the mother, the masculine guarantees a child's physical development. Having to back the one she transformed into
father, femininity, in a complementary manner, guarantees a
child's psychic integrity and spiritual development.

The status of father does not carry with it bodily modification,
but is embodied in the name given to the child, only taking form
with recognition of the child. In one's mother tongue, the name
is responsible for one's actual identity. It provides a central axis to
the development of one's character and person. It provides the
first anchor with which a person grounds himself in language and
articulates the representations he has of himself. Guaranteeing
psychic identity, the family name opens the door to language and
building an identity.

While the father's virility must acknowledge the child as the
product of his acts, the mother's femininity must indicate to the
child that he does not originate solely in his mother's body.
Acknowledgment of the father and the fact of carrying his
father's name allow a child to conceive of his existence in a space
larger than that of the body, the space of language and, therefore,
the space in which the mind evolves. One's mother tongue exists
prior to birth and outlives death. It therefore provides psychic
existence with a force that transcends the body's mortality and
links a life's purpose to the evolution of the species. Recognizing
one's father as a place of origin thus guarantees a psychic potential that differentiates humans from animals. While the maternal

is responsible for cohesion of the body, the paternal is responsible for cohesion of the mind. That is why the paternal image focalizes beliefs about the immortality of the soul. With the development of monotheistic religions, God became a representation of the origins and could no longer be represented with feminine traits. As a result, religions recognize the father as guaranteeing psychic identity and subject the mother's femininity to the father.

Masculinity and femininity uphold the parental positions and are interwoven with them. This support system is undoubtedly indispensable to reproduction and the survival of the species, but also carries with it a certain danger of inhibiting actual sexuality. To the extent that paternity and maternity represent a finality, they cannot serve as a driving force for genital sexuality. On the contrary, they only curb it.

Although parental images preside over a child's sexual development, although they guarantee morality and propriety, although they keep coming back unchanged from generation to generation, they nevertheless oppose the full expansion of sexuality. Contrary to the stand taken by certain religious ideologies, limiting the goals of genital sexuality exclusively to procreation holds many dangers. Doing so implies forgetting that prior to being at the service of the species, sexuality plays a role in a being's psychic regeneration. In this respect, the interplay between virility and femininity remains the only directing force capable of regulating the emotional dialogue between two people and positioning the individuals in their own lives. Therefore, genital health is irremediably linked to the complementarity between masculinity and femininity.

In the Guise of a Conclusion and a Few Words about Oedipus

I have in no way exhausted all the questions arising from sexuality in general and male sexuality in particular. Above all, I have tried to show how a man develops his sexual identity, focusing on a male child's oedipal development. From one chapter to the next, I endeavored to explore the different facets of Oedipus because, generally speaking, Freud's contributions in this area have been poorly understood, by both professionals and the general public.

When a theory is only partly true and disciples grab hold of it, curiously only the most obscure and arguable points are hauled up to the rank of dogma, becoming fetishes of the profession's sorcerer's apprentices. Freudian theory met this fate.

Let's take a closer look. The strong points of the theory are as follows:

1. It considers that words play a nourishing role, like a placenta, in psychic and sexual development.

2. It puts forth that a succession of stages—oedipal, latency, and adolescence—govern this development and oppose each other in the diversity of their goals.
3. It postulates that parents occupy a primary role in the formation of sexual fantasies.

Yet Freud contradicts himself on this third point. On one hand, he situates the father as the privileged support for the ideals that allow a boy to structure his sexuality. On the other hand, he advances that this same boy only dreams of one thing: killing his father to take his place in the maternal bed.

This point led a large number of psychoanalysts to believe in the necessity of parental severity, which they considered to be the only effective obstacle to a boy's incestuous desires. I hope to have shown that this point of view is entirely unacceptable. Moreover, a father following this enunciation to the letter would only encourage his son to develop masochistic, sadistic, or homosexual fantasies.

Of course, Freud could not theorize everything. He did not elucidate the formation of sadistic fantasies, nor the way the unconscious also integrates the parents' unconscious. He viewed sadism as a component of a death wish, a desire to disappear, when the process by which fantasies are formed is everything but a desire to disappear. A battered child validates his father's sadism by integrating it into his own sexual development precisely in order not to disappear. In the secrecy of his fantasies, he says, "I know the hitting hurts, but what incredible power my father deploys in order to love me."

Freudian theory also provides no approach to the way the unconscious structures itself based on the progenitors' unconscious. The fact that oedipal theory, in its original formulation, does not take into account that fantasies incorporate into sexuality various things the parents were unable to resolve in their own lives makes the theory insufficient.

Here is Freud's explanation. He viewed men's dreams of making love to their mothers as translating the truth of a pure and simple desire, rather than seeing the resurfacing of a child's question about the mother's femininity or the father's virility. As a result, he added a castration complex to the Oedipus complex, explaining that the fear of being castrated by the father provides the only counterbalance to a boy's incestuous desires. I have set myself off from Freud's justification of the concept by reformulating the castration complex in light of the true male difficulty: "How to be one with one's sex?" However, I don't think that we can entirely eliminate the castration complex because, above all, it translates the little man's difficulty in assuming his biological sex as soon as words are lacking.

Aside from the gaps natural in a developing concept, the Freudian concept of sexual dynamics neglected two major points. First of all, it neglects the period that precedes the oedipal stage, in which the fetus and the baby develop the sexual orifices. Secondly, it neglects all the aspects of the oedipal period that aim at integrating not only the existence of sex but also the existence of death.

In this book, I did not want to delve deeper into the questions that bind sexuality to lineage, death and, at the same time, illness, not because I have done so in my previous books, but because coming back to it here would have doubled the size of this book. Filial relationships and unconscious transmission between father and son become more complicated because they do not involve any relationship to the body. The bond of common blood relies on the nourishing, placental role words play in psychic and sexual development, much more than in the mother–child relationship. Moreover, as we glimpsed with autism, illness plays an unavoidable role in spiritual development and the integration of death. The curing of a serious or mortal illness, a cancer or a delirium often provides an individual with a springboard to an astonishing spiritual evolution that releases sexuality from the harmful bonds it had to parents and ancestors. Considering the importance of the subject, I prefer to treat paternity, illness, and death in a later book.

In the same way, I did not treat the formation of orifices in early infancy. I hesitated at length on this point, because it allows an entirely new perspective on the mechanisms of erotic pleasure. But because this subject concerns both men's and women's sexuality, I also thought it preferable to reserve this subject for another book.

References

Dumas, D. (1985). *L'Ange et Le Fantôme*. Paris: Editions de Minuit.

——— (1989). *Hantise et Clinique de l'Autre*. Paris: Aubier.

Freud, S. (1909). Two Case Histories. *The Complete Psychological Works of Sigmund Freud*. Vol. 10. London: Hogarth Press, 1955.

Gay, P. (1984). *The Bourgeois Experience, Victoria to Freud: Education of the Senses*, Vol. 1. New York: Oxford University Press.

Heroard, J. (1971). Extraits du *Journal*. *Nouvelle Revue de Psychanalyse* 19: 281–320.

Spears, R. A. (1991). *Slang and Euphemism*. Second revised edition. New York: Signet, Penguin Books USA.

Index